The Golden Girls

T0302635

TV Milestones Series

Series Editor
Barry Keith Grant, Brock University

TV Milestones is part of the Contemporary Approaches to Film and Media Series

A complete listing of the books in this series can be found online at wsupress.wayne.edu

THE GOLDEN GIRLS

Kate Browne

TV MILESTONES SERIES

Wayne State University Press Detroit

© 2020 by Wayne State University Press. All rights reserved. No part of this book may be reproduced without formal permission. Manufactured in the United States of America.

ISBN 978-0-8143-4564-1 (paperback)
ISBN 978-0-8143-4565-8 (e-book)

Library of Congress Control Number: 2020931210

Wayne State University Press
Leonard N. Simons Building
4809 Woodward Avenue
Detroit, Michigan 48201-1309

Visit us online at wsupress.wayne.edu

To Bernardine Smith (1925–2009)

CONTENTS

Acknowledgments ix

Introduction 1

1. Dorothy: Queering Desire through Performance and Performativity 13

2. Blanche: Uneasy Mother and Unruly Woman 34

3. Rose: Promise and Failure of the American Dream 49

4. Sophia: A Trickster Using Storytelling for Good 66

Conclusion 84

References 87

Episodes of *The Golden Girls* Referenced 91

Index 93

ACKNOWLEDGMENTS

I loved telling people that I was writing a book about *The Golden Girls*. Their eyes would light up, and they would tell me a story about watching the show during college or after school with their grandma, or how much they like catching the reruns in syndication. Fandom brings people together, and I'm grateful for all the fans of *The Golden Girls* who make this work worth doing. My name is on the cover, but this was truly an ensemble production.

I am grateful for the Popular Culture Association/American Culture Association for providing space at their annual conference to share the first iteration of this work and allowing scholar-fans to revel in what's possible when we bring our research to bear on our favorite media. I also appreciate the feedback and support of the Wayne State University Press editorial board and staff at every step of the process. Many thanks to Marie Sweetman and Barry Grant for their enthusiastic support and guidance. I am also grateful for the two anonymous reviewers who helped strengthen my arguments in each section of this manuscript. Special thanks to Annie Martin at Wayne State University Press for her encouragement and for keeping in touch.

Supporting a writer is a labor of love, and I'm glad to have had some of the most generous people on my side during this project. Thank you to my family for writing time and space. To Drew and Duncan, always, for the confidence and infinite reasons to write. Finally, to Maren, whose magnitude of knowledge on *The Golden Girls* far surpasses anything I could ever hope to achieve. Our conversations always return to the mystery of doublers, plot holes, and existential quandaries about Stan and the monkey. May we grow old together and never stop laughing about the "Get It While It's Hot Erotic Bakery." Thank you for being *my* friend.

Introduction

The first four notes of Andrew Gold's hit pop song "Thank You for Being a Friend" signal the start of an episode of *The Golden Girls*, a steadfast television companion from 1985 that has aired in syndication ever since. The breezy, string-based reprise sung by Cynthia Fee serves as both the show's theme song and exposition explaining the relationship between four women living together in Miami, Florida. The accompanying shots of an airplane flying at sunset and the Miami skyline echo the song's next line, "traveled down a road and back again." These still shots are followed by a montage that introduces the "Girls"—Bea Arthur as Dorothy Zbornak, Rue McClanahan as Blanche Devereaux, Betty White as Rose Nylund, and Estelle Getty as Sophia Petrillo. The opening credits end with an establishing long shot of the exterior of the house before light orchestral transition music takes viewers from the outside to the inside of 6151 Richmond Street, solidifying the metaphor of coming home that extends into the beginning of each episode. Dorothy, Rose, Blanche, and Sophia are never together in the same room at the same time at the beginning of an episode, so each opening scene begins with one of the women entering the house, the kitchen, or the lanai with an exclamation, a question, or an exasperated observation. The primary plot then begins when one of the women seeks the counsel of the others to solve a conflict that originated elsewhere, such as disappointing news at work, the death of a friend, or a promising romantic evening that turned out to be a dud. In each episode, the four friends help each other navigate the complexities and triumphs of their lives at midlife and beyond, creating a chosen family that network television had never seen before.

The Golden Girls began as a joke. During a promo sketch for the police procedural *Miami Vice* debuting in the fall of 1984, comedian Selma Diamond had a one-liner based on misunderstanding the title as a reference to Florida as a popular retirement destination. "'*Miami Nice*?' It must be about a bunch of old people sitting around playing pinochle" (Harmetz 1985). NBC president Brandon Tartikoff suggested that this type of series would be easier to cast because it did not rely on a handsome but hard-to-find leading man. He continued to develop this idea after watching the 1953 film *How to Marry a Millionaire* and decided to commission a show with a similar premise about "a group of women sharing an apartment together, waiting to meet Mr. Right" (Colucci 2016, 6), and when producers Paul Witt and Tony Thomas pitched an idea for a more traditional family sitcom series, Tartikoff passed. He asked if they would be willing to pitch him *Miami Nice* instead. According to Witt, their charge was to create a show about older women living together. "Society has written them off, has said they're over the hill. We want them to be feisty as hell and having a great time" (6). Witt and Thomas initially balked at writing *Miami Nice*, convinced that NBC network executives would never actually put the show on the air, but Tartikoff insisted. At the time, he had the unenviable job of saving NBC from a ratings slump and attempted to revitalize the lineup with *The Cosby Show*, which premiered in the same 1984 season as *Miami Vice*. Eager to push the limits after winning over audiences by producing a sitcom featuring an upper-class African American family, "the time was right to be daring" (6). Tartikoff's suggestion that a show about older women enjoying satisfying social lives would be "daring" illustrates how mainstream network television prioritizes the needs and experiences of its target demographic of white, economically advantaged young adults.

Witt and Thomas worked with Susan Harris, a creative collaborator and writer, to develop the pilot script. Harris had experience developing the kind of unconventional television Tartikoff wanted including *Soap*, a parody of soap operas that featured an openly gay character, and "Maude's Dilemma," an episode of *Maude* that brought national attention to abortion through a sitcom. She brought the same enthusiasm for challenging social conventions to her treatment of *Miami Nice*, which she retitled *The Golden Girls*, starting with the ages of the characters. Harris recalls getting stuck on the description of the women as "older," which she understood as sixty to seventy but that the network defined differently. "'Older' to them meant women in their 40s, which was astonishing to me because I think that's what I was at the time" (Hunt 2017). Harris and the network compromised by making three of the characters in their fifties and one character, Sophia, a full generation older. The tension between the network's definition of "older" and Harris's experience as an older woman mirrors the way *The Golden Girls* offers a subversive interpretation of aging through the sitcom genre.

For women in mainstream U.S. culture, aging represents not only a loss of vitality but a loss of beauty and desirability. Having lost their youthful beauty, older women (and their concerns) become invisible, a stereotyping that Kathleen Woodward calls a "double aging." She explains that women experience aging as both a biological process and a cultural process of internalizing negative attitudes and assumptions about aging that are "understood in terms of decline, not in terms of growth and change" (1999, xiii). While women may not feel old at fifty, cultural expectations about how that age should impact the trajectory of their lives dictate that they should begin a steady decline. The premise of *The Golden Girls* is funny because we do not expect women in their fifties and beyond to experience growth or desire personal fulfillment. We see the effects of internalized ageism in the pilot episode as Dorothy relates her experience talking to young colleagues in the teachers' lounge. She says she had such a good time with them that she forgot her age and instead "felt like one of the girls." Getting into the car at the end of the day, she was shocked by an old woman—her reflection—in the mirror. Immediately after this scene, Blanche enters to ask Rose if she could borrow a pair of earrings for her date and uses the collective term of endearment "girls." After Dorothy's story, it seems that "the Girls" gestures toward recapturing youth as a way to make sense of the ways in which the show disrupts expectations for what older women should prioritize in their lives. Together and as individuals, the women of *The Golden Girls* defy ideologies of cultural aging by making visible older women's lives that are grounded in renewal and self-discovery.

As a network sitcom, *The Golden Girls* has to function within generic conventions that limit its subversive possibilities, and this could explain why it has been not been more thoroughly considered as having a major impact on the culture of television. Brett Mills notes that the connection between an audience and what they find funny must exist in codified forms like sitcom because "humor relies on the relationship between the teller and the audience for effects" (2005, 8). This means that the comedic premises and jokes within the sitcom genre presume to reveal some truths about who the audience is and what they believe about their world. The shows that scholars choose to study typically fall into broad categories that, taken together, trace a particular historical or cultural moment. If a show is not typical enough to be considered a "normal" example, it may be studied for its radical or noteworthy status outside those parameters, but many sitcoms like *The Golden*

Girls have not been considered exceptional enough (2009, 11). Mills also suggests that the popularity of a show could be a detriment and may deter scholars from studying it based in part on academic elitism, though he suggests being cautious not to allow popularity to overtake other considerations when choosing a sitcom to study (12). As Deborah Jermyn notes, "*The Golden Girls* has most typically been understood as syrupy American sitcom fare" (2009, 45), referring to maligned conventions of television production and commercialization in which sitcoms are often reduced to a vehicle for selling primetime advertising rather than a text worthy of serious critical consideration.

The classic network era that spanned from the mid-1940s to the late 1980s is considered a period that shaped and crystallized the production conventions and distribution methods of television shows according to the commercial purpose of efficiently selling advertisements (Mittell 2010, 10). Major brands interested in buying advertisements on television wanted to reach the standard audience demographic of those aged eighteen to thirty-four, so sitcoms developed a narrative style intended to appeal to everyday people who could relate to ideal families and collegial workplaces. When critics and scholars dismiss *The Golden Girls* as a typical sitcom, that designation carries the baggage of being uninspired and derivative. Gerard Jones summarizes a general attitude about sitcoms as strictly commercial programs with a sinister-sounding motive: "Because [the sitcom genre] creates feelings of warmth and security and positive regard for modern life, it's a perfect shill for a sponsor's products" (1993, 6). Jones links the development of the sitcom to the capacity of television to promote postwar consumerism as the depiction of ideal family life could inspire viewers to model their own lives after their favorite TV family. This focus on the desires of advertisers formed many narrative and production conventions that made the sitcom a predictable and easily replicated genre in the classic network era.

Many of *The Golden Girls*' most powerful symbolic elements are the result of pragmatic conventions of sitcom production rather than intentional choices driven by the script. The opening credits were created in a standard style that compiled B-roll footage and prerecorded scenes from the show to introduce the cast and the key production team. The three-camera studio production style offered a cost-effective way to make sitcoms by using stock sets, but this also led to what the show's production designer, Ed Stephenson, called "the proscenium theater problem," a reference to the way that multicamera sets functioned more like three-wall sets with a proscenium fourth wall rather than a more realistic approach from all angles "but still need to look like someone's house" (Colucci 2016). Stephenson's choice of a pastel color palette and distinct "Florida" style moves the interior away from Blanche's family home to a space that all share equally. To create distinct individual characterizations, *The Golden Girls* relies heavily on script and character development with costumes that establish each of the women as independent of each other while maintaining visual counterpoints when they are together. Dorothy dresses in heavy, draping layers while Blanche wears bright, saturated colors in slim silhouettes. Rose tends toward modest skirt sets and whimsical sweaters. Sophia has a stylized look of an elderly woman with stockings, bland neutral colors, and classic accessories like glasses on a chain and a cameo brooch. The show's designers created an iconic look and feel that remains one of its most outstanding qualities.

The desires and motivations of advertisers formed narrative and production conventions that resulted in cost-effective and easily replicated sitcoms in the classic network era. Any aberration from this proven formula represented too great a financial risk unless the alternative—like losing significant market share—called for desperate measures. Concerns about portraying the lives of unmarried, unrelated older women on a primetime sitcom revolved around whether or not the show would appeal to young adults and, by extension, how this unusual domestic configuration would impact its capacity to generate advertising revenue. A headline from the *New York Times* alludes to the show as a "gamble" for NBC, noting that "the most surprising thing . . . is that nearly everybody is sure the show will be a hit" (Harmetz 1985). Using television shows as a commodity to connect viewers to advertisers has been the economic reality of television since the development of the genre as it evolved from radio, but that does not necessarily diminish the quality of the program. Media buyer Paul Schulman purchased ad time on behalf of his client Ralston-Purina, a pet food brand, because he believed that the show would be popular among the coveted eighteen to thirty-four demographic. "When the show's being taped, audiences stand up and applaud those four terrific ladies for two minutes," he observed (Harmetz 1985). Luckily for advertisers like Ralston-Purina, *The Golden Girls* was an immediate hit, beginning with a standing ovation at the preview screening and regularly earning top viewer ratings in the anchor slot for NBC's Saturday night lineup. After its debut, critics called the show "incorrigibly funny" and "the glorious best of the new season" (Hall 1986). The adoration continued, and over the course of its seven-season run, *The Golden Girls* was rated as a top program for six of those years, earning sixty-eight Emmy nominations, eleven Emmy awards, four Golden Globe awards, and two Viewers for Quality Television awards. It became the second show after *All in the Family* to have all leading ensemble actors win an individual Emmy, a feat that has only been achieved one other time since (by *Will & Grace* in the 2000s).

The Golden Girls remains one of the most popular sitcoms in television history. It is also a show that makes bold choices about portraying marginalized people and the issues they faced in the late twentieth century with empathy and humility. But it is also highly formulaic, overly sentimental, and often careless when engaging with important social issues like the AIDS crisis, immigration, homelessness, and drug abuse. Even the basic hook of the premise that older women can still have fun, satisfying lives relies on dull stereotypes of aging like sagging skin and weight gain. *The Golden Girls* is deeply embedded in practices of television as a commodity industry, but effective execution within this context made it possible to explore complex social and cultural shifts emerging in the late twentieth century. The show's popularity was made possible by conforming to standard tropes and production conventions, and, in turn, its commercial success allowed the show to reach viewers with subversive representations when they mattered most. Mills insists that sitcoms can be "traditional *and* groundbreaking, serious *and* funny, straightforward *and* complex" and that these complexities "should be acknowledged at all times when thinking about sitcom" (2009, 13). *The Golden Girls* has often been dismissed as too closely conforming to a commercial sitcom for critical analysis or too popular to be taken seriously as radical television, but it is worthy of attention because bridging these complexities through characterization made it possible to reach new audiences well into the twenty-first century.

The Golden Girls succeeds at reaching what David Marc calls the "oceanic middle" of standup comedy on which sitcom comedy derives by conforming to rules of social consensus while demonstrating an awareness of social consciousness (Marc 1997, 38). The show's representation of four independent, unmarried, older women who have robust social lives with varied interests simultaneously acknowledges and challenges the social norm, but the structure of the ensemble feels familiar as a family sitcom. Although sitcoms with four-friend ensemble characters are commonplace now (e.g., *Designing Women*, *Seinfeld*, *Girlfriends*, *Sex and the City*, *Will & Grace*), a four-woman friend group living together in the same house as roommates has not been attempted since *The Golden Girls*. The ensemble structure is unlike a family sitcom with a hierarchy that defines the relationships of the group, nor is it a workplace sitcom where the characters are drawn together based on a place or institution like school. To establish their relationship as roommates and friends, the show relies on character archetypes to create a complete ensemble. Anne Kaler argues that these archetypes succeed because together they represent the Jungian concept of the complete woman, an "essential recognition of the complex four-fold nature of human personality, typified by each of the characters—virgin, spouse, mother, and wise woman" (1990, 51–52); Kaler assigns each of the main characters a Jungian archetype. The equality of all four women representing part of a whole woman is a way to make sense of an otherwise subversive domestic situation, but this approach flattens nuanced characterizations into gimmicks. Specifically, this book focuses on the ways in which Dorothy, Blanche, Rose, and Sophia have been overlooked as sitcom stock characters (the smart but ugly one, the slut, the ditzy blonde, and the old-world grandmother, respectively) and highlights the sharp social commentary they make when they complicate these tropes.

This interdisciplinary and intertextual approach to analyzing *The Golden Girls* joins existing scholarship that focuses on archetypal representations of feminine sexuality, representations of aging in television, and the maiden/whore dichotomy (Kaler 1990; Macey 2008; Grant and Hundley 2007; Küpper 2015; Ann 2016; Kannen 2016; Patterson 2016; Van Bauwel 2018). Plot structure, characterization, and language impact broader cultural conversations raised within the chapters. Christyne Berzsenyi suggests that a script-based analysis of *The Golden Girls* is justified for its use of storytelling to "present serious topics, construct character identities, and create intimacy and community among the characters and their viewers as the aging characters mix fantasy with memory to share with, teach, and entertain each other and viewers alike" (2010). As a visual medium, television also conveys messages about identity and representation through costumes, staging, pace, and editing best analyzed using television studies and film theory.

My arguments are also informed by cultural studies disciplines that intersect with discourses of the body including age studies, gender studies, and disability studies. Further, I situate myself as a scholar-fan, and this work continues a thread in cultural studies scholarship that seeks to stake a claim in fandom to reflect the ways that popular culture circulates and to challenge "the myth of the critic as a disinterested and wholly detached reporter" (Dow 1996, xiii). As such, I invite fans to continue their close reading of *The Golden Girls* using new analytical tools and scholars to consider deeper meaning in a text often written off as a derivative and uninspired sitcom.

Each of the chapters that follow explores how the characters Dorothy, Blanche, Rose, and Sophia move beyond their archetype and shows how this complexity makes a powerful statement about women's shifting identities into the late twentieth century. I also argue that this complexity allows each character to negotiate her position within a social or cultural expectation in a way that defies easy categorization. Chapter 1 explores how Bea Arthur, as an established theater and television actor before *The Golden Girls*, lends a queerness to the character of Dorothy that complicates the archetype of "the smart but ugly one," leading to a richer, more developed comedic character. For example, by manipulating the "undesirable" characterization of Dorothy through singing in the episode "Journey to the Center of Attention" (S07E18), this episode highlights the characterization of femininity as a desirable trait for Blanche and complicates Dorothy's usual archetype by overlapping theatrical performance with gender performativity.

Chapter 2 challenges Blanche's identification with the slut archetype by counterbalancing her primary identification as a symbolic and biological mother. Using Mikhail Bakhtin's concept of carnival, I argue that Blanche represents the female grotesque as always in a process of becoming. Blanche defies social norms of motherhood and aging through her contentious relationships with her children, preoccupation with maintaining a youthful appearance, and sexual habits that are both conservative and untethered. When Blanche moves beyond a characterization that is simply "the slut," she makes a powerful statement about how women who raised their families according to midcentury expectations navigated shifting identification with domesticity, motherhood, and sexual liberation at the end of the twentieth century.

Although Rose is often called a "ditzy blonde" known for telling outlandish St. Olaf stories, chapter 3 focuses on how often she made smart, stable choices but is ultimately failed by every institution that promised to protect her. She experiences the same financial anxieties in the pilot episode as she does in the final episode, as well as multiple setbacks and challenges that threaten her financial stability. Rose reflects the same concerns as those of "The Silent Generation," who grew up, raised families, and approached retirement age in the 1980s and faced the consequences of political and economic circumstances beyond their control.

Finally, chapter 4 analyzes the role of Sophia beyond her easy characterization as a colorful, old-world storyteller. When most fans of *The Golden Girls* describe Sophia, they mention her Sicilian roots, outspoken nature, and advanced age as primary attributes. Sophia is arguably the most stylized character of the four women—everything she does is just a little outlandish. I argue that Sophia occupies the role of the trickster by existing both as part of and outside the narrative. She sets the tone, delivers punchlines, and determines morality. This metaphor materialized through the 2010 DVD collector's edition box set when all seven seasons were packaged in a reproduction of Sophia's purse.

I conclude with a look forward to how *The Golden Girls* continues to function as culture-in-progress. From its network run and multiple syndication opportunities to inclusion on television streaming services like Hulu, fans have never been without *The Golden Girls*, but as viewing habits have changed so has sitcom criticism. Fans who consume television through binge-watching or what *Breaking Bad* creator Vince Gilligan calls "a giant inhalation" (qtd. in Oberman 2016, 120) are more likely to notice narrative inconsistencies or aberrations in character development. For *The Golden Girls*, common fan debates include how many children Blanche has, conflicting stories about how Blanche lost her virginity, and the troubling use of "doublers," a fan-created term for actors who play different roles in multiple episodes. For example, actor Harold Gould plays both Rose's beau Arnie Peterson in season 1 and long-term boyfriend Miles Webber in seasons 4–7. "Doubler" can also refer to a single character played by more than one actor; for example, Shawn Schepps and Debra Engle both played Blanche's daughter Rebecca. The proliferation of "wikis," or user-generated information databases, allows character profiles and plotlines to be outlined, collected, and analyzed in ways that did not have to be considered by the show's creators during its original production. Wikis, fan forums, and social media accounts enable fans to engage with the show in a way that allows it to recirculate beyond its original purpose as singular episodes. In this way, *The Golden Girls* and other television shows created in the pre-Internet era exist as more than cultural artifacts and continue to evolve alongside new media forms.

The Golden Girls holds its place as a TV milestone for both its classic sitcom style and its enduring impact on popular culture. Because it continues to reverberate with meaning as it has been taken up by emerging digital media forms, our nostalgia for the show has not diminished as it continues to circulate and shape popular culture in new ways for new audiences. In fact, fan communities continue to grow on social media and through performance events like drag shows, pop-up brunches, trivia competitions, and fan meet-ups. *The Golden Girls* belongs to both classic network television and the landscape of emerging media, conformity, and subversion in equal measure, redefining that familiar feeling of coming home.

1

Dorothy

Queering Desire through Performance and Performativity

The Golden Girls simply wouldn't be without Bea Arthur. Creator Susan Harris wrote the role of Dorothy Zbornak specifically with Arthur in mind. Harris remained so committed to her vision that none of the other actors who auditioned, including veteran Broadway star Elaine Stritch, could alter the character enough to move away from Dorothy as "a Bea Arthur–type"—acerbic, intelligent, and opinionated (Colucci 2016, 18). Arthur started her career in the 1960s acting in off-Broadway theater, leading to her breakout role as Yenta the matchmaker in *Fiddler on the Roof* on Broadway. She transitioned to film work by reprising her Tony award-winning performance as Vera Charles in the film version of *Mame* and to television in a two-episode guest appearance on Norman Lear's *All in the Family*. Lear was impressed by her performance as Maude Findlay, Archie Bunker's liberal, antagonizing neighbor, and he developed the series *Maude* (1972–78) as a starring vehicle for her (17). Harris, known for her unconventional characters like gay Jodie Dallas on *Soap*, took advantage of the offbeat, bracing character traits that Arthur plays so well to create Dorothy as the anchor to the ensemble.

Dorothy is typically described as a divorced substitute teacher originally from New York City with a signature dry wit that can make her seem aloof or standoffish. She has an imposing visual presence that is exaggerated by costuming that emphasizes Arthur's height. Despite the Florida heat, Dorothy usually wears a layered look of wide-leg pants, tunics, oversized tops, and slouchy boots. As a friend, she responds to social situations intellectually and prides herself on having all the right answers when giving advice. She has a close relationship with her family including her mother, Sophia, even though she had put her in the infamous Shady Pines retirement home. In two different flashback episodes, we see Dorothy as a young mother (Lynnie Greene) visiting her parents, Sophia and Sal (Sid Melton). Her ex-husband, Stan Zbornak (Herb Edelman), is also a frequent, if often unwelcome, presence in her life. In the vaudeville-style comedy so often used in *The Golden Girls*, Dorothy plays both the straight man and the comic, alternating between setting up the punchlines with stoic seriousness and delivering them with expert timing.

Dorothy represents the "intelligent warrior goddess" according to Anne Kaler's interpretation of the Jungian archetypes each of the main characters portray in order to comprise a "complete woman"; Arthur's height is a symbol of strength and power (1990, 52). In her one-woman show, *Bea Arthur on Broadway: Just Between Friends*, Arthur claims that she was a shy child because she literally stood out at "five-foot-nine-and-a-half in my stocking feet at eight years old" and that despite being quite shy and reserved in real life, audiences know her for the assertive women she plays on television. *Maude*, Arthur's most significant television project prior to *The Golden Girls*, took a more pointed jab at American politics in ways that other early feminist TV programs like *The Mary Tyler Moore Show* shied away from. *Maude* dealt with topics usually considered too controversial for primetime such as domestic violence, mental illness, and drug laws; in "Maude's Dilemma," a two-part episode also written by *The Golden Girls* creator Susan Harris, the show addressed the issue of abortion (Beale 1992). As the star of *Maude*, Arthur proved a solid and capable leader in a sitcom that tackled serious topics, and this would serve her well when *The Golden Girls* engaged with important social and cultural issues such as homelessness, gay marriage, domestic violence, the AIDS crisis, and assisted suicide.

However, Arthur's political trailblazing on a primetime sitcom came at a cost: her popularity declined, and she acquired a reputation for not being like more traditional leading women in television. A *Time* magazine review suggests a connection between real life and sitcom, noting that "if Actress Arthur is not exactly garden-variety glamourous, Maude [Findlay] is even less likely as a heroine of a TV situation comedy" ("Big Bea" 1973). Yael Kohen suggests that *Maude* departs from the groundbreaking work of *The Mary Tyler Moore Show* for the way that Maude Findlay represents a stereotypical feminist matriarch (2013, 57) while Mary represents "the feminist ideal incarnate, a young, attractive, single woman who supported herself by working in an office and spent her downtime hanging out with friends" (72). Maude is older, thrice-divorced, and aggressively sharp-tongued. Network executives discovered that Arthur was not very popular with television audiences because of her work on *Maude*. "Of the people who knew her, only 20% liked her" (Colucci 2016, 17). The challenge was on for *The Golden Girls* producers, who had to not only convince Brandon Tartikoff that Arthur could carry the show but also convince audiences that Dorothy Zbornak could be much more charming than Maude Findlay without losing her wit or assertiveness.

At the start of the series, it seemed that Arthur would bring the same combative judgment to her role as Dorothy Zbornak that she did to Maude Findlay. In the opening scene of the pilot episode, "The Engagement" (S01E01), Dorothy charges into the kitchen where Coco (Charles Levin), their live-in cook, is making dinner. The very first lines in the show are a tirade against the unconventional look of some of her high school students: "I taught a class today—the finest school in Dade County. Two girls had shaved heads and three boys had green hair." When Coco suggests that the students were just expressing themselves, Dorothy replies, "Well, I expressed myself. I told them they had to leave. They were too ugly to look at." The irony of this opening exchange is that Dorothy's unconventional, "ugly" appearance would anchor the punchlines of nearly every one of the insults directed at her. Despite the jarring start to the series, Arthur quickly found the balance in portraying Dorothy as an opinionated, intellectual critic as well as a compassionate friend, and this dualism came to define the strongest component of her character. Far more than just "the smart but ugly one," Dorothy occupies the role of the leader of the ensemble, taking on more masculine qualities for which she is simultaneously revered and rejected. The "ugliness" Dorothy is often criticized for is a reflection of the expectations for women to always be attuned to physical, emotional, and psychological requirements for attracting and gaining the approval of men as romantic partners. This can include—as it does for Blanche—a hyperfeminine personal aesthetic and a preoccupation with being the kind of woman who can attract a man.

Like other female-driven sitcoms, *The Golden Girls* relies heavily on plotlines that center around the pursuit of romantic relationships. Other shows that used this conceit like *The Mary Tyler Moore Show*, *Laverne & Shirley*, and *That Girl* focus on young, conventionally attractive, never-married working women. *The Golden Girls* features older, sexually active women whose desire is not necessarily confined to a committed, monogamous relationship. Each of the women experiences different kinds of sexual and romantic relationships ranging from flirtations and casual flings to engagements and marriages. This means that their desire for sex is not defined by the kind of relationship they have with a man but by the sexual experience the relationship provides. Although so many jokes focus on her ugliness, abrasive personality, or mannish appearance, Dorothy enjoys several meaningful dating relationships: a brief fling with Don (Terry Kiser), a George Harrison impersonator ("The Commitments" S07E16); a promising but brief off-screen courtship with officer Geoffrey ("Take Him, He's Mine" S02E03); and an affair with married Glenn O'Brien (Alex Rocco, "That Was No Lady" S01E14 and Jerry Orbach, "Cheaters" S05E22). Dorothy's steady success at starting new relationships challenges the notion that only Blanche, Rose, and Sophia can have sexual and romantic relationships because they attempt and ultimately succeed in embodying feminine ideals. Dorothy's marriage to Blanche's cousin Lucas (Leslie Nielsen) during the two-part series finale ("One Flew Out of the Cuckoo's Nest" S07E25/26) succeeds when Blanche's, Rose's, and Sophia's engagements and marriages fail.

Dorothy's alleged inability to attract a man because of her ugliness is well-documented. The barrage of insults about Dorothy's looks resulting in a lackluster dating life seem constant, coming most pointedly from her mother. After Dorothy, Rose, and Blanche are arrested for prostitution and miss a chance to meet Burt Reynolds in "Ladies of the Evening" (S02E02), Sophia chastises Dorothy for her attitude about how the night unfolded. "Jealousy is a very ugly thing, Dorothy. And so are you in anything backless." When Dorothy tries to quit smoking, Blanche suggests that she wean herself off cigarettes by smoking only after sex like she did. "Good idea," Sophia quips. "One pack'll last her a lifetime" ("Sophia's Wedding: Part II" S04E06/07).

Blanche and Rose also insult Dorothy's body when she asks them for advice on her appearance. In "And Ma Makes Three" (S03E20), Blanche and Rose argue about who is the best candidate for fashion show chairman. Dorothy appears in an all-white suit dress to go on a date with Raymond (James Karen), a man she has been seeing for a few weeks, and asks for her friends' advice on which necklace best complements her outfit. Blanche and Rose bicker about the merits of the silver chain versus the pearls when it comes to minimizing Dorothy's "turkey-like neck," "nonexistent bosom," and "huge spare tire jutting out over those square, manly hips." When Dorothy suggests that she instead wear a sign that reads "too ugly to live," Blanche asks whether she will hang it from the chain or the pearls. "Neither! I'm gonna spray paint it on my hump!" Equating ugliness with physical deformity is a running theme throughout the show that reinforces stereotypes about beauty, normalcy, and body image. Blanche and Rose regularly alter their appearance and often go on crash diets, try anti-aging techniques, and upgrade their beauty regimens to include the latest trends. Dorothy gestures toward similar rituals like wearing makeup for a date, but more overt efforts read as awkward and strained. Comedian Harvey Fierstein says that in scenes where Dorothy tries to flirt or act in a feminine way like Blanche, "it's like watching an elephant trying to sit delicately down on a flower" (Colucci 2016, 293). Dorothy's intelligence dominates at the expense of her social skills, but this characterization has a more profound effect on the range of gender performances that she enacts compared to Blanche, Rose, and Sophia.

Dorothy is often called on to take on more masculine roles that involve cross-dressing performances such as Turkey Lurkey ("Henny Penny—Straight, No Chaser" S06E26) and the sheriff ("The Actor" S02E14) when Rose and Blanche are allowed to maintain their characteristic femininity by playing typical female characters created within the world of the play. In "An Illegitimate Concern" (S05E18), Sophia convinces Dorothy to enter the Shady Pines Mother-Daughter Beauty Pageant with her to "put Gladys Goldfein in her place." This presents another opportunity for Sophia to dig at Dorothy's looks when she suggests that her daughter is more beautiful than Gladys's while referring to Dorothy's sister Gloria. Sophia makes it clear that Dorothy is the only choice, and not the best choice, to win a beauty competition. Sophia and Dorothy enter the contest and ask Rose to accompany on the piano to rehearse their act for the talent competition. The live studio audience laughs at the reveal when Sophia enters dressed as Sonny Bono followed by Dorothy dressed as Cher, complete with lip-licking smirk and signature hair toss. This is the only time in the series when Dorothy plays a female character in the context of a staged performance to capitalize on the comic effect of the height difference between Sophia and Dorothy that mimics the visual of Sonny and Cher. This suggests that Dorothy's gender performance is more creative than simple binaries (man/woman, on-stage/real life) and that performativity is always enacted in service of what the performance aims to achieve rather than a strict adherence to the norm. Arthur's ability to move gracefully through theatrical and gendered performances lends a queerness to the character of Dorothy Zbornak that results in not only a richer, more developed comedy but also a more elevated politics for the entire show.

Sophia as Sonny Bono and Dorothy as Cher. "An Illegitimate Concern" (S05E18)

In "Henny Penny—Straight, No Chaser" (S06E26), Dorothy becomes the producer of the spring play to encourage children at her school to read over spring break. Unfortunately, Dorothy's colleague and the play's director, Frank Nann (George Hearn), breaks the news that the first-graders originally scheduled to perform in *Henny Penny* all came down with the measles and need to be quarantined. Dorothy suggests instead that the play be recast with adults after realizing that Rose possesses Henny Penny's sense of "childlike naivete." When Blanche enters the room and mentions that she has not seen Frank since "that weekend in Pensacola," he knows she will be right for the role of Goosey Loosey. Having cast two of the main roles, the only character left is Turkey Lurkey, and Frank suggests that Dorothy might play the part well. She initially resists but then says that she once did a production of *Show Boat* in high school. Sophia pushes her to sing, complimenting her performance by claiming, "No one can sing 'Ol' Man River' like my pussycat." In the next beat, Dorothy sings a line from the song, hitting the famously low bass notes popularized in Paul Robeson's version with ease and then exclaims, "I still got it." When it is time for the performance, Rose and Blanche appear as characters that clearly read as feminine (a hen and a goose, respectively), while Dorothy's costume is all black with a dark purple vest. With a bookish seriousness and Arthur's low alto voice, the character of Turkey Lurkey reads as male. It seems that this version of Turkey Lurkey is modeled after the same character from the 1943 animated film *Chicken Little* (an alternate name for the Henny Penny story), but there is no explanation for why Dorothy's Turkey Lurkey is a male character in this version of the story. The campy humor lands because of the classic three-bit reveal where Rose enters followed by Blanche, so Dorothy's incongruous cross-dressing serves as the punchline of the joke. This is important because it shows that Dorothy's masculinity is a fundamental component of her character, not just a drag bit played for laughs.

Dorothy out of place as Turkey Lurkey. "Henny Penny—Straight, No Chaser" (S06E26)

Gender and theatrical performance overlap when Dorothy is cast as an extra in a play. In "The Actor" (S02E14), Blanche is excited that the Miami Community Players have secured popular television actor Patrick Vaughn (Lloyd Bochner) for their unnamed spring production. Rose, Blanche, and Dorothy share her excitement and fawn over Patrick, each proclaiming in turn how attracted they are to him. When he arrives at the theater, they all decide to audition for the role as his leading lady. After the auditions the women are cast as nonspeaking townspeople. They are noticeably disappointed. Before they leave the theater, Patrick makes a date with each of the women, giving different reasons to each of them why they shouldn't tell the others about the special bond they share. The scenes that follow are a madcap farce as Patrick tries to keep each of the women from finding out about his dating the others. Finally, the night of the performance arrives, and a stagehand comes in to tell Patrick that the actor originally slated to play the sheriff has come down with the flu. Dorothy is recast in that role because she is the only one who fits in the costume. Cross-dressing seems like a throwaway bit, but at its core is the incongruity of Dorothy as a traditionally feminine character. The last major scene of this episode reveals that Patrick deceived everyone by lying about having relationships with every female cast member while Dorothy is standing on set in the big-bellied sheriff costume. Dorothy would be out of place as a woman in the ensemble of a play ostensibly set in the 1950s. Blanche, Rose, and the other women actors wear feminine, A-line dresses with flowers in their hair, which was a typical portrayal for women in plays set in the period. The same costume on Dorothy would be misaligned with her character, but in the context of the play there would be no role for her if she were not cast as a male-presenting character. The conceit of Dorothy needing to step in to replace the actor down with the flu gives her room to perform masculinity in a way that makes sense within the world created by the play. It is Dorothy's ability to perform, enhanced by the real talent of Bea Arthur, that allows Dorothy to operate in the spaces between masculine and feminine, repulsive and attractive, domineering and subordinate.

Dorothy participates in the "queering" of *The Golden Girls*, a process described by Eleanor Patterson as accounting for not just the presence of gay and lesbian characters in sitcoms but all the ways that shows "make sense of the performativity or signification of non-normative sexualities or gender identities" (2016, 841). Although Dorothy is not a lesbian character, the queerness in her performance of gender identity is enacted through an incomplete performance of womanhood as well as the ways in which the show plays with Dorothy's expressions of masculinity and femininity through theatrical performance. In television studies, reparative interpretations of shows not explicitly produced for a queer audience attempt to "analyze the representation and visibility of sexualities and genders that

Dorothy as "the sheriff" while Blanche and Rose play 1950s housewives. "The Actor" (S02E14)

challenge hegemonic constructs" (Patterson 2016, 841). The construct at work here is the pressure for women to conform to narrow ideal standards of beauty if they are to be considered attractive and desirable. Dorothy's ability to attract partners without this gendered performance sparks the conflict that drives the plot of "Journey to the Center of Attention" (S07E18), an episode that highlights how Dorothy's talent for singing makes it possible for her to define what beauty and attractiveness mean on her own terms.

Blanche's and Dorothy's sexual archetypes as "the slut" and "the smart but ugly one," respectively, are firmly established early in the series. Blanche prides herself on her ability to attract a man and the extraordinary lengths she will go to for a sexual conquest, while Dorothy would rather stay in on a Saturday night (interpreted by the other Girls as a thinly veiled excuse for not being invited on any dates). Blanche admits that her constant focus on sex and her own beauty is an attempt to mask her deep insecurity and that she sometimes feels that Dorothy has a stronger, more confident presence. Because Blanche leans so heavily on her desirability, anything that threatens her identity as sexy to all heterosexual men cuts her to the core. Rose, Blanche, and Dorothy are, despite their close, loving companionship, fundamentally rivals competing for male attention. This rivalry drives many of the jokes that undercut each of the women's beauty or ability to secure a date and affects Dorothy and Blanche's relationship most profoundly.

"Journey to the Center of Attention" begins with Dorothy lying on the couch in her frumpy, maroon pajamas completely absorbed in watching a segment about a corn-shucking device on the infomercial show *Amazing Discoveries*. Blanche emerges from the hallway ready for a date in a semi-sheer, bright blue dress and kitten heels. When she stands next to the couch, the contrast between each woman's idea of a great Saturday night becomes clear. Blanche is dismayed that Dorothy would waste another Saturday night without a date and insists that they go together to her favorite neighborhood bar, the Rusty Anchor. When Dorothy admits that she is uncomfortable with strangers, Blanche says that she shouldn't worry because "they're just as uncomfortable with you" and suggests a self-esteem exercise that might help Dorothy regain some confidence. She sits next to Dorothy on the couch, further highlighting the contrast in their costumes, and explains that the exercise involves saying three positive things about yourself. As an example, she says that she is "beautiful, men find me desirable, and people want to be my friend." Dorothy repeats the three affirmations and Blanche laughs because she believes Dorothy misunderstood the exercise: "I'm sorry I confused you, honey. You're supposed to say three positive things that apply to *you*." Even though Blanche pressures Dorothy into meeting new people and going on dates, she does not view Dorothy as an equal in the pursuit.

Blanche questions Dorothy about her night at home on the couch instead of going to the Rusty Anchor. "Journey to the Center of Attention" (S07E18)

Eventually, Blanche cajoles Dorothy into going with her to the bar. When they arrive, Blanche is embraced by the bar patrons and leaves Dorothy alone to make her own acquaintances. Dorothy sits down at a table with a man who leaves as soon as she arrives. The piano player notices Dorothy sitting alone and asks if she sings. After she demurs and insists that "some people might enjoy making fools of themselves in public, but, me, sing? I don't think so." The piano player continues trying to goad her into singing, finally suggesting "some Irving Berlin." Dorothy agrees, adding, "D flat is good for me." Dorothy's initial hesitation suggests a performance all its own by building up to her identity as a singer rather than revealing her desire all at once. The piano player begins to play the classic Berlin tune "What'll I Do," and after tripping over the beginning lyrics, Dorothy gains confidence and her singing draws the attention of all the bar patrons toward the piano and away from Blanche. She adds a flourish to the final key change and the Rusty Anchor erupts in enthusiastic applause.

During the next scene at the Rusty Anchor, Blanche sits on the bar tying cherry stems with her tongue. The bar patrons chant her name, and when she produces a tied stem, one of the patrons announces that she's tied a Bosun's knot. Blanche tells the crowd that a Star of David will be her next trick and Dorothy walks in the door. The men immediately flock to Dorothy and ask her to sing, leaving Blanche alone and dejected. Dorothy closes the scene with a show-stealing rendition of the songbook standard "Hard-Hearted Hannah." In the final scene at the Rusty Anchor, Rose and Sophia accompany Blanche to see Dorothy sing. This is a departure from the other scenes because Dorothy's earlier performances at the bar seemed improvised, but the final performance is planned. Before Dorothy starts singing, Blanche interrupts and asks if anyone has considered that she might like to sing. She takes off her trench coat to reveal a red, sequined dancer's outfit and starts to sing "I Wanna Be Loved by You" in an affected, sultry voice reminiscent of Marilyn Monroe's popular rendition of the song in the 1959 film *Some Like It Hot*. But the performance is studded with mishaps including Blanche getting tangled in the microphone cord, slamming the piano lid when she sits on top of the piano, and inadvertently sitting in the lap of a man who just had hip surgery. The performance is a disaster and Blanches runs from the bar visibly shaken.

Dorothy finds Blanche in the bathroom, where she finally admits why she came to the Rusty Anchor with the intention to upstage Dorothy:

> BLANCHE: Dorothy, the one thing in my life I've always been assured of is being the center of attention. Oh, I knew I never had to worry about competing with any other woman 'cause I'd always win. But when I saw you sing the

Dorothy captures the attention of the Rusty Anchor singing "Hard-Hearted Hannah." "Journey to the Center of Attention" (S07E18)

> other night, I realized why all those men were practically fallin' all over themselves to get to you. Because, Dorothy, when you sing, you light up the room. You do. You positively glow. You're just—you're beautiful.
>
> DOROTHY: Oh, Blanche, you don't have to say that.
>
> BLANCHE: Well, believe me, I don't like sayin' it. But it's true. You can attract men in a way I can't and I'm jealous of you.

In this moment, Blanche reveals the difference between her interpretation of ideal femininity and Dorothy's performative gender identity. Blanche perceives her sexiness and ability to attract men as a core component of her personality rather than a choice or skill set that can be activated at will, but her performative femininity is equally complex. Dorothy enters a space of active attraction when she sings and uses it to her advantage when it suits her.

The magnetism of her performance at the Rusty Anchor draws the attention of the same men who previously focused exclusively on Blanche's hyperfemininity. The complexity of her ability to attract, manage, and relate to others is made possible through a nuanced performance of gender identity that is often shown most clearly through the context of theatrical performance. Eleanor Patterson's suggestion that "queering" can work to make sense of performativity helps frame Dorothy's gender and theatrical performances. Costumes allow Dorothy to move in and out of performative spaces within both the metanarrative of the performance and her characterization in the show. The producers of *The Golden Girls* recognized that Arthur's costumes needed to reflect a more masculine aesthetic to reinforce the jokes and her role as the leader of the group. Her clothes were custom-made with draping silhouette designed to almost completely conceal her body (Colucci 2016, 333–34). Even during episodes when the women attend banquets, dances, and other formal occasions, Dorothy always wears floor-length gowns or suit dresses with wide-leg palazzo pants. Richard Schechner argues that performance is a ritualized, culturally specific way of expressing identity and that when the actions of performance become ritualized as identity markers, these actions become "performative." He adds that performativity is very broad, "a whole panoply of possibilities opened up by a world in which differences between media and live events, originals and digital or biological clones, performing onstage and in ordinary life are collapsing" (2002, 110). This blending of identity and repetitive social action makes performativity both distinct from and dependent on performance and has more to do with constructing identity through the process of ritualization rather than the behaviors themselves. This means that "natural" identities comprised of behaviors and actions taken for granted as part of everyday life can be considered performative in their effects.

French philosopher Simone de Beauvoir posits that "one is not born, but, rather, becomes a woman" (1974, 301). She asserts that "woman" is a set of behaviors, practices, rituals, and physical markers that, taken together, produce gender identity and that this is not something bestowed in the natural order but rather a learned performance. Each person learns to perform a specific gender identity through "vocal inflections, facial displays, gestures, walks, and erotic behavior as well as how to select, modify, and use scents, body shapes and adornments, clothing, and all other gender markings of a given society" (Schechner 2002, 131). Feminist theorist and cultural critic Judith Butler built on de Beauvoir's argument to suggest that gender performance is based on emulating social rituals aligned with binary gender representations. She explains that gender is "a stylized repetition of acts . . . which are internally discontinuous . . . [so that] the appearance of substance is precisely that, a constructed identity, a performative accomplishment which the mundane social audience, including the actors themselves, come to believe and to perform in the mode of belief" (1990, 45). In other words, gender can be taken for granted as "natural" when it is actually a series of stylized choices that, taken together and repeated regularly, create an illusion of "man" or "woman." Over time, the accepted definitions of "man" and "woman" become the norm, so that anyone who deviates outside of those boundaries is portrayed as not fitting in. Blanche signifies this performativity whenever she says that she needs to change her clothes in order to go on a date. However, performativity is not limited to constructions of a single gender and, in fact, may do its most powerful work when the boundaries between genders are blurred past the point of easy identification. Dorothy often occupies space in this gray area by speaking, moving, and dressing in ways that mix feminine and masculine identity markers to suit the situation. This complex gender performance is enhanced in *The Golden Girls* by many moments of theatrical performance that show Dorothy (and, by extension, Bea Arthur) to be comfortable performing multiple identities for specific purposes.

The gender complexity of Dorothy's character aligns with Arthur's own involvement with gay rights activism, for which she was well known. Arthur acknowledged that her politics influenced character choices in her career, saying Maude and Dorothy shared her liberal viewpoints. *The Golden Girls* continues to circulate as a touchpoint for gay culture for pioneering sitcoms with gay characters who were specifically distanced from deviant stereotyping. Prior to *The Golden Girls*, gay sitcom characters were frequently limited to single-episode cameos like Steve from *All in the Family* or were wildly stereotypical characterizations like Jodie Dallas on *Soap* (Aronstein 2012). Even though the writers' original concept for Coco included him being a drag queen, Charles Levin insisted on portraying the character without the "swish" of the gay stereotype. Coco appeared only in the pilot episode, cut due to the complexity of writing for five main characters and because having a live-in cook made the four women seem more well-off, confusing the premise that they cannot afford to live independently (Colucci 2016, 34). But having a gay character who did not read as *gay* set the tone for other episodes in the series that treat LGBTQ issues in a measured, nuanced way without relying on prejudicial tropes. This exposure to gay, lesbian, and transgender characters who have strengths and flaws without the deviance associated with non-normative gender expressions or sexualities allowed viewers to see variant identities in an approachable way. Dorothy's friend Jean (Lois Nettleton) visits after the death of her partner, Pat, and shares her story of grief after her relationship of eight years in "Isn't It Romantic?" (S02E05). Clayton Hollingsworth (Monte Markham) has difficulty coming out to his sister Blanche in "Scared Straight" (S04E09) and returns to Miami to marry his long-time partner Doug (Michael Ayr) in "Sister of the Bride" (S06E14). These characters experience love, loss, and friendship just like Dorothy, Blanche, Rose, and Sophia do, and these plotlines work as "paraexposure," or the transfer of empathy to LGBTQ people in real life after being exposed to characters on television that defy stereotypes (Schiappa et al. 2006, 15). Arthur championed gay rights, and showcasing LGBTQ characters in *The Golden Girls* left an indelible mark that opened up new possibilities for gay representation on television.

Although Dorothy's characterization pushes the boundaries of traditional portrayals of women on television, *The Golden Girls* regularly distances its characters from lesbian connotations. Mimi White argues that shows like *The Golden Girls*, *Designing Women*, and *Kate & Allie* based on women living together as family while making it clear that the characters are not lesbians establishes "women's bonding as a form of social stability, a viable and attractive alternative to the traditional family" (White 1987, 162). *The Golden Girls* regularly uses "lesbian episodes," jokes, mistaken identities, and double entendre to reinforce their relationships as homosocial instead of homosexual. Alexander Doty suggests that this method disarms what he calls "the lesbian charge," or the accusation that the women's relationships with each other as "just friends" are "fully distinct from (as well as preferable to) the homosexual through another network of jokes that work to contain, disempower, or devalue visible representations of lesbianism" (1993, 43). In "Foreign Exchange" (S04E24), Blanche and Rose take a "dirty dancing" class and it is quickly discovered that Rose is the better dancer. Blanche feels determined to prove that she can perform just as well as Rose, and they practice their couples' choreography in the living room. Near the end of the routine, Dorothy and Sophia enter the room but are unseen by Rose and Blanche until the song ends. Startled, Blanche reassures Sophia and Dorothy that their dance was not sexual in nature. As they start to rearrange the furniture displaced by their rehearsal, Sophia takes Dorothy aside to tell her, "What they do is their business, but if I ever see your hand on Rose's behind, it'll kill me." The joke that Rose and Blanche dancing together could be considered lesbianism is diffused by Blanche's reassurance that "this is not what it looks like." A queer reading of Sophia's assertion that "what they do is their business" allows, as White and Doty suggest is possible, an interpretation that Sophia acknowledges that lesbian attraction and intimacy is acceptable but not for her own daughter.

"Isn't It Romantic?" (S02E05) and "Goodbye, Mr. Gordon" (S07E15) do the heavy lifting to make sure the women are clearly read as heterosexual by dealing with another character's lesbianism (Jean, a high school friend of Dorothy's) and a case of misidentification, respectively. While anything less than a full subversion of cultural expectations may dissatisfy some audience members and critics who would have liked *The Golden Girls* to go farther as a role model for queer identities on TV, the show's treatment of non-normative identity and issues facing the contemporary queer community does important work to bring these issues to mainstream television audiences. Not only does the show feature beloved side characters with varying queer identities, their characters are fully developed and never rejected from the women's family or social circles. Each of the characters is connected to a gay, lesbian, or transgender character, and these relationships help audiences recognize and embrace the role of queer friends and family in their own lives (Schiappa et al. 2006). Not only do these characters appear onscreen, they have the opportunity to tell their own story. This "restorying" (Berzsenyi 2010) makes it possible for these characters to situate themselves within the home community and become agents rather than having stories told about them to others.

As a cultural product in-progress, *The Golden Girls* can be read both as an artifact and as influencing change, so these multiple lenses impact various interpretive queer readings. The academic field of performance studies provides some insight on how formal, theatrical performance and everyday performances overlap and converge in a way that explains how Dorothy fulfills multiple conceptual roles. Rather than thinking about performance strictly as acting or creating a character, performativity suggests ways in which context shifts our actions and behavior to conform to or subvert social and cultural expectations. In this way, Dorothy's multiple performances both within the context of a creative performance and through the generative repetition of prescribed gender roles highlight the many possibilities for self-expression. Arthur's performance as Dorothy Zbornak made an important contribution to the scope of gender representation on television by presenting a relatable, fully developed character who takes a lead role in her own life.

2

Blanche

Uneasy Mother and Unruly Woman

In the pilot episode of *The Golden Girls*, Rue McClanahan plays southern belle Blanche Devereaux as demure and thoughtful with only a hint of the provocative sexuality that would come to define the character throughout the series. She sweeps into the kitchen wearing an off-pink silk dress and diamond earrings to ask Dorothy if she can borrow her mink stole for an important date. In this scene, Blanche is coquettish, not sexually aggressive, but self-absorbed in her own vanity. Over the next few episodes, McClanahan found her stride, emphasizing the sensual, bawdy characteristics that make Blanche stand out in the ensemble. In contrast to Dorothy's characterization of sexuality and gender as a complex performance, Blanche's entire identity seems to revolve around sex and attracting men through idealized femininity. This certainly rings true in her fandom as handmade crafts and T-shirts quip, "Dorothy in the streets, Blanche in the sheets." Her entrance into the story arc of the show involves an engagement to Harry (Frank Aletter), a man who would prove to be a bigamist by the conclusion of the pilot, and she spends the next seven seasons in search of Mr. Right Now. By the third episode of the series ("Rose the Prude" S01E03), Blanche's sexuality becomes the punchline for the show's first slut-shaming joke. In the episode, Rose feels unsure and nervous about the possibility of having sex with beau Arnie Peterson (Harold Gould, who would later play Rose's long-time boyfriend Miles Webber) for the first time since her husband, Charlie, died fifteen years earlier. Blanche expresses deep shock and dismay that Rose has not had sex in over a decade, but she is rebuked by Dorothy. "Oh, back off, Blanche! Not everyone is classified by the navy as a friendly port." And so begins the first in an almost constant barrage of sex-themed insults and plotlines for Blanche, the slut.

The term "slut" first appeared in Geoffrey Chaucer's *The Canterbury Tales* meaning a "dirty, slovenly woman," but its pejorative application as an insult referring to a promiscuous woman can be traced to the late medieval period (Westcott 2011). The ideology around the term "slut" reproduced by *The Golden Girls* centers on the dichotomy between "slut" and "good girl" as defined on television through functions of hegemony, or the way that institutions like commerce, government, and the media shape and control moral ideology (Dow 1996, 9). Audiences are supposed to understand that Blanche is a slut because of how many men she dates no matter how much she discloses about her sexual proclivities. Rose is a "good girl" because she follows the rules of monogamy. In "Son-in-Law Dearest" (S02E23), Dorothy, Blanche, Rose, and Sophia talk about infidelity, and Rose tells the story of when she suspected Charlie of cheating when he came home from work one night and went straight to bed. After exchanging confused looks, Rose explains that for the first eighteen years of their marriage, she and Charlie had sex every night and every morning. "Charlie said that's why we didn't have headaches and we both had really shiny hair," she explains. Within the context of monogamy, Rose's sexual activity, no matter how frequent, is not considered deviant.

Blanche is consistently labeled a slut, a term she never challenges and almost wears as a badge of pride. In "Old Boyfriends"

(S07E14), Rose receives a visit from Thor Anderson (Ken Berry), a high school boyfriend from St. Olaf. But when he arrives, Rose realizes she does not remember him and asks Blanche to help ask him questions that might jog her memory. Blanche seems perplexed that Rose would have difficulty remembering an old boyfriend and Rose explains that she could not remember him because she had fifty-six boyfriends in high school. "Of course," she explains, "that was before I knew Charlie. I probably would have had more, but I wasn't allowed to start dating until I was a senior." Here, the definition of what a slut is becomes unclear as Rose and Blanche argue about whether or not you can have a boyfriend "without having to go all the way." Blanche is genuinely hurt when Dorothy calls Rose "the Grand Pooh-Bah of Slutdom" because she equates the label of slut with successful conquest and proof of her attractiveness. Blanche is less concerned with adhering to ideals of appropriate sexual behavior than she is with making sure she is always the most desirable woman in any room. The turnaround joke on Rose's admission of fifty-six boyfriends in just her senior year of high school implies that she would have had many more if her father had allowed her to date. This short conversation and its comic premise reveal some of the guidelines for determining appropriate sexual behavior for women. First, Rose obeys her father's rules about dating, and then does not "go all the way" with her boyfriends. She is offended that Dorothy calls her a slut because of the number of boyfriends she had because, according to the rules, the line that divides a "good girl" from a "slut" is clearly defined according to emotional and sexual monogamy. Obviously hurt, Blanche tunes out of the conversation only to blurt out later in the scene, "*I'm* the biggest slut!" This callback reinforces the incongruity of Rose and Blanche as foils, one rejecting the slut label and one embracing it.

Blanche revels in her slut identity, and the comedy derived from it reflects what Mary Russo calls the "female grotesque" (1986, 219). Drawing from literary theorist Mikhail Bakhtin's concept of carnival, or the upending of traditional social rules and expectations for behavior, Russo argues that "the laughing hags" violate social norms by "making a spectacle of themselves" through inappropriate exposure of their bodies. Blanche represents the grotesque by speaking loudly, frequently, and with great demonstrative flourish about her sex life. She dresses provocatively, takes great pride in her appearance, and goes to great lengths to conceal her true age. She is unashamed by her desire and often laughs after she has been made the punchline of a slut joke (220). This laughter works in the service of establishing Blanche as an "unruly woman," defined by Kathleen Rowe as a comedic character in television and film who uses grotesque laughter "to challenge the social and symbolic systems that would keep women in their place" (2011, 3). Blanche not only resists the slut/good girl dichotomy of sexual politics reinforced by hegemonic television stereotypes but also complicates the role of the sitcom mother. She is not the nurturing, self-sacrificing mother who transitions gracefully to a sexless middle age after her biological children have grown into adulthood. Rather, she embodies Bakhtin's "pregnant, senile hag" (2009, 26) as she is in a constant state of becoming and reinvention. Blanche challenges the notion of what a mother can and should be, violating both sexual expectations for older women and the role of sex in the life of a mother.

Throughout the show, Blanche is frequently described by herself and others as self-absorbed, vain, and capricious. Her actions suggest that she is extremely selfish and finds it hard to empathize with others facing adversity that does not involve conflict with a romantic partner. What we know about Blanche's past suggests that she has not changed much since her youth and that her man-crazed midlife is just an extension of her adolescent predilections. Still, Blanche insists that she remained faithful to her late husband, George, throughout their marriage, living with him in the house she now shares with Dorothy, Rose, and Sophia. In this way, Blanche occupies the role of incomplete mother—providing and maintaining the domestic places and spaces without the attendant emotional nurturing typically associated with an idealized mother.

Television critics frequently summarize *The Golden Girls* as a show focused on feisty, sex-crazed older women in Miami but single out Blanche as alternately "sex-starved" or "oversexed." Her sexual desire is unusual as "the slut" because of the number of sexual partners she enjoys and the high expectations she has for the men she dates. The prevailing cultural message about women's sexuality is that sexual desire naturally declines with age, and loss of youthful beauty requires that sexuality be put aside. Blanche fights aging not only to appear more attractive to men but also because she believes in the link between youth and sexuality. She goes to great lengths to conceal her actual age, dresses in bright, revealing clothing, and walks with a coquettish gait. Blanche commands attention on screen by standing when others sit, by making sweeping gestures, or by being the first to dramatically walk out of the scene. Blanche's comedy relies less on wordplay and wit and more on the incongruity of an older woman enthusiastically engaging with the drama of life.

In "Blanche and the Younger Man" (S01E09), Blanche meets Dirk (Charles Hill), a young fitness instructor, and embarks on an anti-aging skincare and fitness regimen in order to make herself appear even more youthful to keep him interested in her. As Thomas Küpper notes, this plotline responds to the fitness craze of the 1980s, typified by Jane Fonda's workout series that suggests that women could reclaim their youth through aerobics. The episode is not a mockery of Blanche but instead an effort to highlight the hegemonic compulsion for fitness and youth that Dirk represents, which she ultimately rejects once it is revealed that the reason Dirk felt attracted to Blanche is because he reminded her of his mother (2015, 259). The episodic structure of the sitcom format lends itself to similar cycles of aging and generational conflict of mothers and daughters negotiating role reversals as caretakers, reinforced in this episode by Rose's conflict with her own mother, Alma Lindstrom (Jeanette Nolan), whose visit from St. Olaf is the backbone of this episode's B plot. Alma tells her own story of desire, explaining to Sophia while playing cards that she had a relationship with a much younger farmhand after the death of her husband. The primacy of female relationships in *The Golden Girls* requires the women to navigate roles as mothers, lovers, and caretakers that may not conform to a linear, discrete structure in favor of Bakhtin's "becoming" in a constant reconfiguration of sexual identity.

Although representations of age are important for all of the characters, Blanche is particularly impacted by cultural and biological processes of aging as they relate to how she perceives her sexuality. By concealing her true age and wearing clothes that make her appear younger, she demonstrates that she is aware of how these cultural processes affect her identity. When cultural and biological processes intersect, Blanche has a difficult time orienting herself to a new reality. In "The End of the Curse" (S02E01), Blanche confuses her menopause symptoms with pregnancy. This sets up a joke about how many men Blanche slept with during her fertile period and an admission that it was so many that she cannot identify who the father might be. "That was a particularly active time for me. I looked stunning. I'd had my teeth bonded." Because she still identifies as a young woman, she assumes that the absence of her period means that she is pregnant and worries about how her body will look after having the baby. That Blanche would consider pregnancy as a cause for her symptoms instead of menopause shows how thoroughly she has accepted the delusion of her own anti-aging campaign. Blanche's identification with a mother role has more to do with her youth than any affinity for children. After she returns from a doctor's visit to confirm the pregnancy, she runs directly to her room and refuses to come out. Rose and Dorothy ask if the baby is a boy or a girl. Blanche responds, "The worst thing." Fearing a tragic prenatal complication, Rose and Dorothy assure her that everything will be fine, she will get the best medical care, and they will be there to support her and the baby. Blanche does not reply so they begin to daydream about what college he will go to (Harvard for Dorothy, the University of Minnesota for Rose). When Blanche finally emerges from her room, she breaks the news.

> BLANCHE: I'm not pregnant. It's worse. It's much worse.
> DOROTHY: Blanche, what is it?
> BLANCHE: My life is over.
> ROSE: Oh, Blanche. I'm sorry. I'm sorry for thinking all those bad things about you when I thought you were pregnant. Like what a slut you were for having all those men. The things only a tramp would do. But now that you're dying, please forgive me, I didn't know.
> BLANCHE: I am not dying, Rose, but I might as well be. It's menopause. Well, I wish I could die because as far as I'm concerned, this is the end of my life.

For Blanche, the possibility of pregnancy at her age is not as devastating as the reality that her childbearing years are over. Blanche grieves, but not for what menopause symbolizes as an end to her fertility. Rather, she mourns the loss of her youth and ability to attract men. She falls into a deep depression, and after a week the other Girls insist that she see a psychiatrist. Dr. Park (George J. Woods) tries to help Blanche understand that menopause does not mean the end of her sex life.

Blanche admits that menopause represents aging and that this means that she has lost a core component of her personality. Eventually Blanche realizes that menopause does not mean that her life is over or that she has to give up on the sex life she enjoys so much. She credits her friends more than Dr. Park for helping her out of her depression: "I know that beauty like mine cannot fade overnight. He didn't have that much to do with it. It was you girls. You let me go and be crazy and you were right there. . . . You were caring and supportive and I thank you for it. I'm lucky to have friends like you." Blanche labels her "crazy" as excessive, hormonal emotion, but she is not singled out or ostracized. Instead, she is supported through a difficult time by her friends. Her perception of diminished sexual capacity is not dismissed as unimportant but rather acknowledged and affirmed as a core component of identity, a loss that is treated seriously by her friends. As such, the central theme of motherhood plays out through Blanche's character development in complex ways, adhering to and subverting stereotypes of women's roles within a family.

Blanche has a contentious and often conflicted relationship with motherhood, and this is an issue that frequently appears in her plotlines. In "Second Motherhood" (S01E19), she faces another marriage proposal, this time from Richard (Kevin McCarthy), a wealthy business owner. To Blanche, there's a catch: Richard has two school-aged children. She balks at the idea of being a mother figure to these children and feels some dismay at the thought of having to relive that time for the benefit of her would-be husband. She admits, "I just hate myself for feeling this way, but I don't want to be a mother again. I mean, it was a wonderful experience at the time, but I always thought this part of my life was supposed to be for me." Blanche's perspective pushes back on the concept of the ideal woman as someone who is always ready and willing to step in to provide emotional labor. She consistently subverts this expectation by affirming her desires through a commitment to living her life on her own terms. What could be construed as selfishness suggests a commitment to liberated living and an unwillingness to compromise on the ideal of midlife as a time for self-exploration for the sake of a partner. Blanche's primary allegiance is to her own pleasure and how her pleasure helps support her role as a romantic and sexual partner for the men in her life.

Blanche's fractured commitment to motherhood as a lifelong occupation rather than a discrete period of caregiving runs counter to the characterization of motherhood seen in the other Girls. Dorothy shows affection toward her two children, Kate (Lisa Jane Persky and Deena Freeman) and Michael (Scott Jacoby), and still plays an active, somewhat overbearing role in their lives. Sophia and Dorothy are a mother-daughter pair, and although their relationship is strained at times (most critically around the issue of Sophia's stay at the Shady Pines retirement home), we read Sophia and Dorothy's relationship as close and loving. Rose fondly remembers the experience of raising her children, and also maintains friendly relationships with them. Her sons Biff, Skippy, and Doug never appear in any episode, but Blanche's daughters Janet (Jessica Lundy) and Rebecca (Shawn Schepps and Debra Engle) appear in episodes with plotlines based on long-standing mother-daughter conflicts. Janet and Blanche communicate their disagreements most frequently on the phone, but the narrative arc that most clearly establishes Blanche's fractured mothering centers around Rebecca's journey to motherhood. The three-episode arc represents Rebecca at three stages of motherhood—pregnancy, childbirth, and as a single mother—and Blanche is forced at every turn to renegotiate her identity as a mother and witness to Rebecca's experience.

Rebecca, often called Becky, makes her first appearance in "Blanche's Little Girl" (S03E14), an episode that marks her return home after being away for four years. Blanche explains that she and Rebecca had a huge fight after Rebecca decided to leave school and become a fashion model. Predictably, Blanche compliments her daughter's beauty as her defining characteristic. "Gorgeous blonde hair, sparklin' blue eyes, a figure men would mortgage a house for. We were always so much alike." When Rebecca arrives, Blanche is shocked to discover that she has ended her fashion career after gaining a substantial amount of weight and is cruelly tormented by her verbally abusive boyfriend, Jeremy (Joe Regalbuto). Although Blanche finds herself disappointed with the direction Rebecca's life has taken, she does not want to alienate her daughter by interfering in their relationship. However, her protective instincts cause her to confront Rebecca about her low self-esteem after Jeremy proposes, which leads her to end their relationship.

Rebecca returns for the narrative arc that illustrates both Blanche's ambivalent feelings about motherhood and her uneasy transition to the role of grandmother. "The Accurate Conception" (S05E03) opens with Rose preparing breakfast for Blanche and Rebecca (now played by Debra Engle), who is visiting for the first time in many years. Blanche delights in having Rebecca at the house, happy that the two can finally bond after another unexplained fight that kept them apart. Blanche takes breakfast to Rebecca on the lanai, where she explains that even though she would like to stay and visit longer, she needs to get back to Atlanta. When Blanche presses her for details, Rebecca feels reassured by their promise to no longer keep secrets from each other and secure enough in their relationship to share that she has an appointment at a clinic for an artificial insemination procedure. Blanche reacts poorly, asking, "Why would you do something like this? Just to hurt me?" Rebecca feels attacked and betrayed because she thought she could be honest with her mother only to find that Blanche cannot accept her choices without judgment. Blanche does not respond with compassion or curiosity. Instead, she focuses on how Rebecca's chosen path to motherhood might affect her (Blanche). Blanche later admits that her objection is based not on the process of artificial insemination or Rebecca's decision to have a child but on her lack of a husband. For Blanche, Rebecca's failure to secure a husband reflects poorly on her as a mother who should teach her daughter to prioritize marriage before having children. For Rebecca, motherhood represents a true choice and a means to structure her family in a way that makes sense to her.

Blanche eventually comes to terms with Rebecca's decision and attempts to support her by accompanying her to the sperm bank. Blanche and her friends make jokes about test tube sons-in-law, and Blanche continues to dig at Rebecca. "I just cannot believe you are actually gonna give money to someone like this sperm pusher. You are a Devereaux. A Devereaux has never had to pay for it." Jokes and snide comments soon drive Rebecca out of the clinic, as she feels frustrated and misunderstood. At the crisis point after Rebecca decides to return home early, Dorothy helps Blanche understand that the conflict is not really about artificial insemination but allowing her daughter to make her own decisions and take control of her life. Blanche reconciles with Rebecca at the final moment before she leaves for the airport and makes the rare gesture of apologizing for her behavior.

Rebecca returns for two more episodes after the artificial insemination plot, "Blanche Delivers" (S06E01) and "Even Grandmas Get the Blues" (S06E20). In "Blanche Delivers," Rebecca returns to Miami for a short visit before the birth of her baby. Although Blanche has conditionally accepted Rebecca's pregnancy and decision to raise her child as a single woman, she still worries about what the doctors at the hospital will think of her daughter's unconventional choices. Rebecca further antagonizes Blanche by revealing that she intends to have her baby in a holistic birthing center instead of a hospital. "They emphasize natural childbirth in a relaxed atmosphere with no painkillers," she explains. "First Becky conceives in a clinic, now she wants to deliver in a bedroom. She's got the whole thing backwards."

Birthing centers developed in response to the rise of lay midwifery in the 1970s (Feldhausen 2000), so Rebecca's choice represents her engagement in countercultural discourse on childbirth and the tension between her and her mother's generational attitudes about childbirth. However, hegemonic order is eventually restored after the women accompanying Rebecca make a disastrous and alarming visit to the birth center that makes Rebecca decide on a hospital birth. In the delivery room, Blanche realizes that her desire to control Rebecca's family narrative has divided them and puts aside the conflict to help her daughter through labor. "Rebecca Devereaux, I think you must be about the bravest woman alive. . . . Honey, I couldn't do what you're doin'. You've got courage I never had. Why, you just decided how you wanted to have your baby, and you're doin' it. I think that's wonderful. I'm just so proud of you." This moment reveals that Blanche has a difficult time connecting to her emotions surrounding motherhood because of her preoccupation with the judgments of others. This insecurity is mirrored in her attitudes about aging and concerns about how she will be perceived by the men in her life, as she often sabotages relationships with female family and friends to attract or impress a partner.

In "Even Grandmas Get the Blues" (S06E20), Rebecca—who now lives in Miami due to Blanche's insistence that she be

Blanche's daughter Rebecca visits the birthing center. "Blanche Delivers" (S06E01)

close to family—returns with her new baby, Aurora, and asks Blanche to babysit so that she can go to a job interview. Blanche has her own plans: an audition for the role of Kate in the community players' production of *Taming of the Shrew*. The role is fitting, as Blanche describes Kate as "the fiery tart of Padua who no man could tame" while dressed in a revealing Elizabethan costume. She has no choice but to bring Aurora with her to the audition. Blanche meets Jason Stillman (Alan Rachins), an actor who has recently moved to Miami, after she bombs her audition because she is distracted by Aurora's crying. Jason strikes up a conversation with Blanche and assumes that she is the baby's mother. Blanche realizes that his assumption means that she appears younger than her actual age and does not correct him. For most of the episode, Blanche continues the ruse of being Aurora's mother, even asking Rebecca for a chance to babysit on a day when she has plans to meet with Jason. Blanche pretends that Rebecca is Aurora's nanny, and after Rebecca leaves, Jason alludes to the possibility that he and Blanche could have a baby of their own someday. When Blanche's lie is revealed, Jason immediately breaks off their relationship and Blanche believes this is because she is a grandmother. Jason, however, says that the relationship must end because he cannot trust Blanche, once again confirming to Blanche that it is her looks relative to her age that men find most important. Rebecca, having witnessed the confession and its aftermath, becomes angry and leaves with the baby. Blanche and Rebecca reconcile with Sophia's help recounting the tale of the Feast of the Dancing Virgins as a celebration of mothers and daughters. This narrative arc offers several opportunities to explore themes of caregiving, changing attitudes about how to define motherhood, and complex feelings sparked by life transitions like menopause and grandchildren.

Blanche has a difficult time transitioning to her role as a mother because of the expectation that mothers must sacrifice their individuals wants, needs, and desires for the sake of their

Blanche dressed in her audition outfit. "Even Grandmas Get the Blues" (S06E20)

children. Blanche provides love, comfort, and care to the men in her life, but as long as she is defined by her role as a mother, these relationships hold little weight in establishing Blanche as a caregiver. Yet the balance of power does not fall in her favor as she is often subordinate to their wants and desires, always shaping and molding her physical appearance, demeanor, and attitude to what is likely to please her partners. For Blanche, deviant sexual behavior and her willingness to subvert the rules are limited to what is acceptable behavior within monogamous relationships. While she revels in being called a slut and being known for her sexual prowess, she does not readily accept her daughter's desire to become a single mother or her brother's homosexuality. Labeling Blanche as a slut for her promiscuity and openness about her sexual desire does not mean that she acts without judgment. However, the dichotomous relationship

Blanche is distracted by her granddaughter at the audition. "Even Grandmas Get the Blues" (S06E20)

between the slut and the good girl suggest that women must be one or the other. Blanche represents the complexity of women's shifting identities, desires, and priorities. Her "becoming" resists a linear start and finish, and the comedy of her character comes from subverting cultural expectations and clinging to them in equal measure. Perhaps it is more accurate to say that Blanche is best defined not as a slut but as an "unruly woman" who typifies the disruptive identities available to women in the late twentieth and early twenty-first centuries (Rowe 2011). This disruption allows women to navigate shifts in power and support, disrupting the reliance on the institutions that promise to reward conformity and sacrifices that often fail women like Rose who play by the rules.

3

Rose

Promise and Failure of the American Dream

In 2017, Katie Couric interviewed Betty White on the occasion of her ninety-fifth birthday. Sitting on the couch of the studio set with a sloth stuffed animal Couric brought as a gift, White expressed gratitude for her good health, her mental acuity, and a community of fans and colleagues who continue to support her acting career. "I am the luckiest old broad on two feet," she beamed (Couric 2017). Like many early television actors, White began her career in radio in the 1940s and experienced the rapid development of new styles and formats. Early television programming followed a radio model that relied more heavily on ad-libbing and direct-to-camera talking than scripted fiction (Mittell 2010, 163–64). White's television career began in 1949 when she was hired as the co-host of *Hollywood on Television* with Al Jarvis (the show was originally called *Al Jarvis' Make-Believe Ballroom*), a daily show that began on radio and transitioned to television as five and a half hours of ad-libbed material six days per week. Because of this experience, White is credited as the first woman in television history to host a talk show. After Jarvis left the show in 1951,

White continued to co-host with his replacement, Eddie Albert. That year, she was nominated for a "Best Actress" Emmy, the very first award in a category designed to recognize the accomplishments of women in television. White went on to co-create and star in the sitcom *Life with Elizabeth*, winning a Primetime Emmy in 1952. The show made White one of the few women in early television to have creative control in front of and behind the camera (Kilday 2009).

During the 1950s and 1960s, White continued to work steadily across various formats, including variety shows, talk shows, and game shows, and provided commentary on the live broadcast of the annual Tournament of Roses Parade for nineteen years. Throughout her career, she adapted to new broadcast formats and further developed her craft as an ensemble comedian. She became a darling of the game show circuit and turned a guest role as Sue Ann Nivens on *The Mary Tyler Moore Show* into a full-fledged recurring character. She was a regular guest on variety shows like *The Carol Burnett Show* and *The Tonight Show with Johnny Carson* and acted in several television movies and miniseries (White 1995). By the time she came to *The Golden Girls*, White had established herself as an indispensable feature of network television. In hindsight, the title of her 1995 memoir *Here We Go Again: My Life in Television* is ironic because it implies that *The Golden Girls*, which had recently wrapped production at the time of the book's publication, would be the capstone of a successful, decades-long acting career. Instead, *The Golden Girls* was only the beginning.

White continued to enjoy a robust acting career after *The Golden Girls* ended in 1992. Following the short-lived spin-off *Golden Palace* that also starred Estelle Getty and Rue McClanahan, White continued to make regular cameo appearances in films and on television, talk shows, news magazines, and commercials, as well as adapting to new forms like digital streaming video. She held a Sophia-like role in TV Land's four-woman ensemble *Hot in Cleveland*, and in 2010, at age eighty-eight,

White hosted *Saturday Night Live* for the first time. Her inextricable link to the fabric of television as a cultural institution is compounded by her contribution to sitcom history in her signature role of Rose Nylund. Rose represents the mythical, all-American, small-town girl, wide-eyed and innocent, naively trusting the goodness in everyone she meets with complete faith in the sacred institutions of family, country, and the free market economy. Rose uses anecdotes to share the mythology of the American dream and the promise that if you work hard, help your neighbor, and follow the rules, everything will be okay. For Betty White, that seems to be the case—a young actress wins the hearts of audiences across the country during the infancy of television, stays committed to developing her craft, and is rewarded with a long and fruitful career in Hollywood. The truth is always more complicated, but America loves a good story.

One of the most well-known conceits of *The Golden Girls* is the St. Olaf story. Told by Rose to share a moral tale, justify her experience, or give advice on topics ranging from romantic troubles to professional crossroads, St. Olaf stories are quintessential folktales. The characters are hearty Midwesterners whose innocent foibles and dimwitted follies reinforce the importance of upholding family values as seen through the lives of a close-knit Norwegian American immigrant community. Rose believes in the fundamental goodness of her fictional hometown of St. Olaf, Minnesota, and its inhabitants. In these stories, she paints charming scenes of snowy Christmases with hot cocoa by the fire, family singalongs, and joyous harvest celebrations that led to the conception of at least one of her children. St. Olaf stories—bucolic, absurd, rambling and full of tangentially related moral lessons—agitate Rose's nostalgia for halcyon days and help establish her character as the perfect rural mother and housewife. She represents the way life ought to be for women with the type of sweet, caring demeanor audiences would recognize from similar rural fantasies of *Petticoat Junction*, *The Beverly*

Hillbillies, and *Green Acres*. Her costumes reflect a casual modesty and are neither provocative like Blanche's nor frumpy like Dorothy's, and she tends to follow rather than lead. Rose often wears childish sweatshirts with teddy bears or airplanes and enjoys games and making crafts. Her use of words that sound Norwegian, such as in "Oh, blow it out your *tubenburbles*!" or in describing the late-night snack of "*sperheoven* crispies," makes Rose sound absurd. However, she can also be self-sufficient, sexually alluring, and aggressively competitive, adding a nuanced complexity that resists a wholesale stereotype.

Jay Sandrich, director of the pilot episode, not only suggested the pivotal change that White and McClanahan switch their original roles but also gave White notes not to play Rose as dumb but naive. "She believes everything she is told and, in her innocence, always takes the first meaning of every word," White explains, adding that she "had her own set of rules that made perfect sense, if only to her, and she also had a fierce Nordic temper on occasion" (White 1995, 249). Rose is also compassionate and generous and has an aptitude for mechanics from growing up on a farm. In many ways, Rose is the most misunderstood and underestimated of all the women, and her naivete reflects her commitment to her strong sense of moral order. Rose follows the rules no matter what, but this conviction also leaves her disenfranchised and vulnerable.

Rose is constantly worried about the security of her future and frequently finds herself in precarious financial situations. In the pilot episode, when Blanche's possible marriage threatens to disrupt their living arrangement, Rose shares her concerns with Dorothy about potentially having to move out and find a new place to live.

> It's not fair, you know. I mean, we get married, we have kids, the kids leave, and our husbands die. Is that some kind of a test? You don't work that hard, you don't go through everything you go through to be left alone. We are alone, Dorothy,

> we really are. Our families are gone and we're alone. And there are too many years left, and I don't know what to do.

Dorothy reassures her that they are not alone because they have each other, and later in the episode they make a pact to take care of each other "no matter what."

Rose's concerns echo the growing frustrations shared by her peers born between approximately 1925 and 1949, sometimes called the Silent Generation, who were defined by their belief in frugality and delayed gratification in exchange for a financially abundant future. This left young adults of the Silent Generation risk-averse when it came time to build their careers. *Fortune*'s story on the "College Class of '49" was subtitled "Taking No Chances": when they went on job interviews, their first questions were about pension plans (Howe 2014). This generation witnessed widespread financial insecurity during the Great Depression and the years leading up to World War II but was also bolstered by the economic boom of the postwar era in the 1950s and 1960s (Timmerman 2005, 30). By the time they reached retirement beginning in the 1980s, many of the social and economic supports that women of the Silent Generation relied on such as family systems and spousal income began to fail through divorce or widowhood, loss of a company pension, or reduced retiree health benefits. *The Golden Girls* shows how women began to adapt by entering the workforce and pooling resources to survive and thrive. Yet, despite making all the "right" choices to ensure a stable midlife, Rose feels these pressures more acutely than her friends.

Rose, Dorothy, and Blanche become roommates because of life circumstances that required them to take more control over their financial futures, and communal housing provided a solution. Blanche, the owner of the house they share, recognized that renting out spare rooms would be an opportunity to increase her income. In "The Way We Met" (S01E25), Blanche reveals that she had another set of roommates prior to meeting

Rose and Dorothy. "Two very eccentric old ladies who used to bathe together and floss each other's teeth. I kicked them out one morning and that very afternoon went down to the supermarket to advertise for new ones." Rose met Blanche in the supermarket, explaining that she was being forced to move from her current apartment. Dorothy simply responded to Blanche's newspaper ad. Fans of the show often describe the relationship between the women as evidence of the bond between friends as a chosen family, but this episode reminds viewers that the women started out as strangers who became roommates, then grew close as best friends who treat each other like family.

Their bond is tested in "That's for Me to Know" (S07E04). Blanche wants to add a hot tub to the house and Rose tells her that she's required to secure a building permit. Blanche refuses

Blanche and Rose meet for the first time at the supermarket. "The Way We Met" (S01E25)

to make the appointment for the permit inspection because she does not want to pay the taxes and fees, and proceeds with her plans to have the hot tub installed. Rose insists on following the rules and reminds Blanche that "the city requires a permit on any new home construction built within five feet of a standing structure used as a primary dwelling." Rose, aware that installing the hot tub without a permit means breaking the rules, calls the code enforcement office without telling Blanche. Don Benson (Richard Stahl) arrives to issue the $80 building permit and when he learns that Blanche rents out rooms in her house, he tells her that she needs a special boarding license. The juxtaposition between the two women is striking as Blanche wears a bright, striped robe and a new swimsuit next to Rose, who is dressed in gray pants, a white button-down shirt, and a green sweater vest. Blanche cheerfully tells the inspector to issue the license on the spot and add the cost to her total bill. He then tells her that the permit is only $40 but that the improvements she would have to make to the house to bring it up to full compliance with the building code as a boarding house would average $10,000. Without the improvements, she would need to evict a renter within forty-eight hours. Rose's insistence on following the rules puts them all in a precarious situation where at least one of them could lose their home. This leads to a difficult conversation and an attempted vote to determine who should leave. Later, Dorothy suggests that they become co-owners of the house. Blanche takes offense. "This is my home we're talking about here. And it's more than a home. It's memories. Dorothy, this is where I lived with my husband. It's—it's my past, and it's my future. As I move on towards middle age, it's all I have." Rose begins to worry about finding new housing like she did in the pilot episode, and both Dorothy and Rose are hurt by Blanche's unwillingness to extend the title when the three women had repeatedly vowed to take care of each other and protect their financial futures. Eventually, Blanche agrees to share the title with Rose and Dorothy because of a renewed commitment to her friends as chosen family.

This episode highlights the tension between loyalty to family of origin and obligation to chosen family and raises important issues of financial security for older women without legal protection for their assets. After she sells her family home in St. Olaf after Charlie's death, Rose has no property rights and her housing depends on Blanche's goodwill. Women who have aged out of the traditional workforce face increased risk of economic instability because of factors such as high out-of-pocket bills for acute health care, the possibility of needing long-term care, Medicaid eligibility, and unexpected inflation in housing costs (Holden and Smeeding 1990, 194). These risks combined with lower overall income, especially for women like Rose who lack relevant job skills and experience, exacerbate the effects of financial insecurity with potentially disastrous consequences. During the time Dorothy, Blanche, and Rose would have been an active part of the workforce, single or widowed women were denied credit, faced major gaps in wages, were limited in the type of work available to them, and had few opportunities for financial independence outside of marriage. Only Dorothy developed a career as a teacher independent of her husband; she even acted as the sole provider for her family during Stan's unstable career as a novelty salesman. Still, she is affected by her husband's decisions including costs associated with their divorce, financial mismanagement resulting in an audit, and neglectful treatment of their shared investment assets. Sophia, Rose, and Blanche fulfilled more traditional roles as wives and mothers and at midlife rely on a mix of economic supports such as Social Security income, part-time employment in addition to their husbands' pensions, life insurance, and retirement savings. These supports were made possible by a family structure in which the husband's career provided not only income during his life but also an institutional assurance that income would be available to his family after death.

Rose's strong family values are clearly demonstrated throughout the show in the way that she speaks about her late husband, children, and St. Olaf neighbors. Friends and neighbors become legends through her detailed retelling of mundane events like "The Great Herring War" and "Gunilla Gets a Catalog." But the institution of marriage fails her when Charlie dies and then again because he failed to adequately prepare for Rose's future without his income. In "The Truth Will Out" (S01E16), Rose's daughter Kirsten and granddaughter Charley visit from Minnesota. Rose tells her friends that she is nervous about Kirsten's visit because she is making Kirsten the executor of her will and has to share some important news with her. When Kirsten arrives, she questions why her mother would live with roommates: "When you first told me you were moving in with some other ladies, I was really surprised. . . . I thought, why would anyone who could afford to be totally independent want to live with someone else?" Rose reveals the basic truth about her financial situation—that she is not financially independent—but lies to Kirsten about the reason. She blames herself for losing the inheritance on bad investments and pyramid schemes that she never actually made to divert Kirsten's anger away from Charlie.

When Dorothy and Blanche enter the kitchen and overhear the argument, Blanche defends Rose, saying that she's not the type to squander money on bad investments. This underscores the reality that Rose's chosen family understands her better than her own daughter. According to Rose, Charlie Nylund was not a very good salesman, so he did not have substantial savings upon his death. Charlie was "the worst businessman ever to balance a checkbook" and did not leave his family with the money that she told her children that he provided. Rose lied in order to protect the reputation and memory of her late husband for the sake of her children and grandchildren, fulfilling the role of the supportive mother and wife in ideal families in sitcoms like *Father Knows Best* and *Leave It to Beaver*. Her children would have been part of the Baby Boom generational cohort that grew up in the 1950s and 1960s, and these shows would be familiar for presenting the gold standard of family life when her children were young (Jones 1993, 123–24). Women like Rose who trusted their futures to safety net systems had to renegotiate their independence in midlife and beyond. Dorothy's suggestion that Rose needs to find her way back to security reflects a common need to adapt to changing economic realities in order to survive.

Even though each of the women faces some financial instability at times as a result of seasonal or sporadic employment, unexpected expenses, or other financial misfortunes, Rose regularly suffers setbacks and hardships that threaten her financial security in a significant way. First, in "Job Hunting" (S01E22), Rose loses her job at the grief counseling center because of funding cuts. Initially, Rose is more concerned about how the clients of the counseling center will get help and even invites a particularly distraught client to spend his days at their home so that he will have somewhere to go. Dorothy reminds her that they cannot afford to live without steady employment: "If we miss a couple of paychecks, we are in big trouble." Job security is a major concern for both women, but Rose seems unbothered by the need to find a new job right away. She does not share her plan to find a new job, and eventually Dorothy accuses her of not trying hard enough. Rose tells them that she has been going on job interviews for weeks but that no one will hire her because of her age. Dorothy reminds her that her chances for securing a well-paying job depend on work experience that Rose simply does not have: "You are fifty-five, unemployed, your husband is dead, and you have no training. Let's face it, Rose. You're not exactly Mary Lou Retton." Dorothy's advice responds to another difficulty faced by job-seeking older women who spent most of their adulthood tending to the domestic sphere: being out of the working world for so long left them without the necessary skills to find employment that would allow them to be financially independent. Dorothy helps Rose revise her résumé and gives her a boost of confidence by reminding her that she has triumphed over difficult financial situations before. Rose blames her inability to get a job on her age rather than on the fact that being a housewife for thirty-two years left her unprepared to enter the job market later in life. Dorothy's suggestion that "the rules have changed" accurately describes the failure of institutional security that many women of her generation learned to rely on. Eventually Rose finds a job as a waitress at the Fountain Rock Cafe, and later in the season Rose returns to work at the grief counseling center when it reopens. But this would not be the last time that an unexpected failure of a supposedly reliable institution would put Rose's future in jeopardy.

In "Rose Fights Back" (S05E04), Rose finds out that the insurance company that Charlie worked for has gone bankrupt and can no longer fund pensions. Even though Rose works as a grief counselor, she has to find another part-time job to make up for the income provided by the pension. She expresses dismay at the situation, explaining that Charlie worked hard so that she would be financially secure: "You know what gets me mad about this whole thing? All those years Charlie put into that job just for the pension. He used to say, 'Rose, I hate selling horseshoes, but if I do it long enough, you'll be set for life.'" This attitude of self-sacrifice shows how young adults of the Silent Generation placed their futures in the trusted hands of institutions that promised to protect them later in life. Women and men entering midlife in the 1980s valued stability and were more likely to endure personal discomfort in the present for the promise of benefits at retirement.

Dorothy describes growing up in this era when she affirms Sophia's accomplishments as a mother in the flashback episode "A Piece of Cake" (S02E25). "You raised three kids during the Depression and always managed to have food on the table. You had two jobs as far back as I can remember but were always there when we needed you." Sacrifice, saving, and waiting to reap rewards later in life are frequent themes for the Silent Generation. According to the timeline of the show, Rose and Charlie would have been born right at the beginning of this period, raising their large family in the postwar era when it seemed like this deferment would pay off. By the 1980s, many women who spent their adult lives supporting their husbands who worked for wages were forced to renegotiate financial independence on their own terms because of divorce or widowhood.

Faced with the uncertainty that the loss of the pension brings, Rose attempts to find another job. She has an interview as an assistant manager at a pet store—the perfect job for an animal lover like her—but is told by the hiring manager that she is too old. Dorothy and Blanche encourage Rose to take this blatant case of age discrimination to Enrique Mas (Chick Vennera), a local television news reporter and consumer advocate. At first, Rose seems too caught up in the panic of the possibility that she will have to move out of the house if she cannot find a job to support her part of the rent to care about fighting the pet store management and delivers a powerful monologue that reflects the core of the anxiety faced by many women in similar situations:

> You know, every morning when I leave the house, I see this bag lady going through the garbage over on 135th Street. She has everything she owns piled in one of those old shopping carts. Well, the other day, for the first time, I noticed she's about our age. You know, you always feel sorry for someone like that, but I wondered, what did she do to get herself into a fix like that? I thought, well, she must be lazy. Or she must be pretty stupid to let something like this happen to her. But the truth is she's me.

The precarity of older women without social and financial supports is clear here, as well as the common misconception that poverty is always a result of personal failings and poor money management. Bolstered by her friends' promise to support her as long as it takes for her to get a job, Rose sets off for a meeting with Enrique Mas. While she waits to have her interview, she finds out that the station is looking to hire a production assistant. When she inquires whether she can interview for the position, Enrique tells her she's not the right fit because of her age. Rose argues that he is attempting to discriminate against her when she came to him for help fighting an age-related employment discrimination issue, and he agrees to give Rose a trial consumer reports assignment. She gets the job but fails to secure a promotion to cub reporter in "Melodrama" (S06E19) when she ineptly but enthusiastically covers the Miami Pet Dog Expo and a robbery occurs during the broadcast. Despite her error in judgment about the robbery as the breaking news story, Rose continues to work for Enrique Mas and eventually receives another promotion and her own assistant after consumer reporting takes its toll on her. Rose learns to advocate for herself at work and develops the skills necessary to thrive.

Rose also finds herself embroiled in important political and cultural issues including nuclear war, drug addiction, and the AIDS crisis. Even though Dorothy is more outspoken about social issues and politics, plots that center around Rose's involvement in broader issues add an unexpected depth to the show's engagement with them. In "72 Hours" (S05E19), Rose receives a letter from the hospital instructing her to report for an AIDS test due to possible contamination in the blood she received from a transfusion during a surgical procedure. Dorothy, Blanche, and Sophia accompany Rose to the hospital to support her during the test, but the doctor tells her that it will be three days before her results are ready. She becomes agitated and angry, telling the doctor that "first you give me that transfusion, and now you tell me this," echoing the sense of betrayal she experienced around Charlie's pension; the institutions she trusted to keep her safe have failed her. Blanche tries to put Rose's mind

Rose interviews a dog owner who is hiding under a table during the robbery at the Miami Pet Dog Expo. "Melodrama" (S06E19)

at ease when she confesses that she has had an AIDS test and has since continued to get tested regularly. Later in the episode, Rose lashes out at Blanche in a way that reveals common misconceptions that many people had at the height of the AIDS crisis of the 1980s and 1990s. She questions why she was put in this situation because "this isn't supposed to happen to people like me. You must have gone to bed with hundreds of men. All I had was one innocent operation." Blanche, hurt by the accusation, reminds Rose that "AIDS is not a bad person's disease" that punishes people for bad behavior. This exchange is significant because it directly references Blanche's increased risk for contracting HIV/AIDS because of multiple sexual partners, but the subtext also refers to the common belief that AIDS punishes gay men, a population disproportionately affected by HIV/AIDS (Scott 2003). Anti-gay prejudices result in the belief that people who contract HIV/AIDS do so as a result of immoral actions: Rose claims that she should be spared from the disease because is "a good person." In the end, Rose's test returns a negative result, restoring the status quo.

Similarly, Rose's sitcom-sanitized challenge with prescription drug abuse in "High Anxiety" (S04E20) reinforces her moral exceptionalism. After Rose enters the kitchen unusually agitated and restless, she lashes out at Dorothy, Sophia, and Blanche as well as the film crew that has arrived to film Sophia and Dorothy for a pizza restaurant commercial. The next day, Rose apologizes for her odd behavior, explaining that she ran out of pain pills. Blanche becomes suspicious and presses Rose for an explanation. Rose says that she takes the unidentified pills for pain after a back injury sustained doing farm work thirty years ago, and when Blanche expresses concern that she has continued to take daily prescription pain medication for that long, she reacts with anger and storms out of the room. Rose clearly resents the implication that she is an addict and insists that she can live without the pills. When her friends find her rummaging through the cabinets in the middle of the night looking for the pills, Rose realizes that she may be dependent on the medication. Her solution is to challenge herself to one night without taking the pills to prove that she can live without them. Dorothy, Blanche, and Sophia stay up with her all night, but her resolve does not hold. After admitting to Blanche that she took a pill a few nights later, Rose enters a recovery treatment center and returns home after thirty days. She insists that she is not cured of addiction but that she can "live without drugs my whole life, one day at a time." Rose's recovery is never addressed again, even when she enters the hospital for heart surgery and needs pain medication in her rehabilitation. Rose vehemently rejects any association with the label "addict" and her substance abuse is treated almost as an accident or a miscommunication between Rose and her doctor. She becomes part of emerging conversations in American culture about the identity of people with HIV/AIDS and substance abuse, and while she never fully aligns with the profile of a person who might be blamed for these conditions (e.g., a gay man or a sex worker), her struggles suggest to audiences that these stereotypical profiles do not accurately represent real people's experiences. Still, quick and uncomplicated resolutions to these problems required by the sitcom genre absolve Rose of responsibility because she is not considered at fault but is instead an innocent victim of circumstance.

Darcie Wilder, reflecting on the "uncanny valley" of "High Anxiety," suggests that this episode reveals an uncomfortable truth about Rose. If she finds it so difficult to get through one night without her pain pills, "this means that every single scene in every single previous episode is altered with the knowledge that she could have been high as a kite. Everything we know to be true about Rose could be a total lie" (2017). *The Golden Girls* scripts were not required to be overly attentive to narrative continuity, and contemporary viewers tend to forget the episodic impact of sitcoms produced before DVD sets and digital streaming services made it possible to consume more than one episode at a time. The argument that Rose's personality is fundamentally deceitful is based on the assumption that the episodes of *The Golden Girls* are meant to be consumed in serial, and it is just as plausible that in the chronological arc of the series—independent of the show's production schedule—that this episode reflects an earlier period in Dorothy, Blanche, Rose, and Sophia's time as roommates. But even if that were not the case, and Rose was in fact forced to reveal her drug addiction over several seasons and after a significant amount of time had passed, the suggestion that her personality before the reveal was a lie betrays a common misconception about substance abuse that is even more relevant to cultural conversations about personal risk and the morality of supposedly deviant behavior. The type of substance abuse profile Rose exhibits is more in line with the addiction portrayed on the cable drama *Nurse Jackie*, a show that features a woman whose prescription drug addiction goes undiscovered by her family and work colleagues for years until her personal life spirals out of control.

The prototypical profile of "the addict" or "the person with HIV/AIDS" as an abnormal identity is based on the assumption that disease is a punishment for undesirable lifestyle choices and used as justification for discrimination. As an innocent victim of the institutions that were supposed to protect her, Rose can remain powerless to her circumstances. *The Golden Girls* shows us that many of the circumstances that carry a message of only happening to "bad" people—poverty, drug addiction, job loss, homelessness, and infectious disease, for example—have no such threshold. Rose supposedly makes all the right choices and still finds herself in situations that she believes are outside of the experiences that a "good," "normal" person should have. As such, Rose Nylund represents the shifting allegiances, creative use of resources, and self-actualized possibilities for older women adapting to new social, cultural, and economic realities in the late twentieth century. Rose as a dumb character remains a victim of circumstance while a naïve Rose has an opportunity to change course, responding to each situation as she continues to learn and grow.

4
Sophia

A Trickster Using Storytelling for Good

Estelle Getty began her career in television as the unlikely cast member of *The Golden Girls*. When she arrived at the first audition, she had never been the star of her own television show or won a major critical award like her costars. Before she commanded the small screen as Sophia Petrillo, Getty performed standup comedy in the Catskills before landing a breakout role as Harvey Fierstein's mother in his Broadway play *Torch Song Trilogy*. As the story goes, network executives knew they wanted to cast Getty right away but were waiting for someone more famous like Carol Burnett to top her in the role. She was called back for round after round of auditions to read with potential castmates without confirmation that she had secured the role. Finally, Getty took matters into her own hands—literally. She created the "old lady" look she knew Sophia should have, and scoured secondhand shops looking for the perfect accessory. When she arrived at that last audition wearing a gray wig and glasses and carrying what would become her iconic straw purse, Getty finally convinced them that she truly belonged in the role of Sophia Petrillo (Colucci 2016, 12).

Getty's only-in-Hollywood story of the plucky actor's rise to fame is a perfect match for her role in *The Golden Girls*. Sophia

Petrillo is rarely content to leave well enough alone, always meddling, complicating relationships, and scheming to get what she wants. Originally from Brooklyn, New York, by way of Sicily, Italy, Sophia brings a stereotypical old-world wisdom and charm to the house. Prior to living with Dorothy, Blanche, and Rose, Sophia lived at the Shady Pines retirement community, or "the home." She arrives unexpectedly during the pilot episode because of a fire at Shady Pines and quickly establishes a reputation for candid observations and one-line zingers. In this episode and most others, Sophia wears a dowdy, crocheted sweater with a lace collar, eyeglasses attached around her neck with a chain, and opaque stockings. She carries a paper bag that serves as her luggage along with her purse and pushes past Dorothy to sit on the couch. But Sophia is more than a quirky grandmother character. She also represents the archetype known as a trickster, a character that manipulates the trajectory of the narrative using mischief for her own gain but who is also driven by a desire to teach the protagonist a lesson. In mythological storytelling traditions, trickster characters function as boundary-crossers that "violate principles of social and natural order, playfully disrupting normal life and then re-establishing it on a new basis" (Mattick 1998). Trickster characters take on a variety of meanings and associated symbols situated within the culture from which they derive such as Norse mythology, Native American folklore, and African American slave narratives. Lori Landay notes that female tricksters like Lucy Ricardo from *I Love Lucy* tend to move between dualisms, "fluidly shifting between different impersonations as the situation dictates or destroying the old self to become a super-self" in order to create a third interpretive possibility (1998, 11). Often, tricksters have an unusual amount of intellect or secret knowledge that can be deployed to make other characters behave in specific ways. This manipulation is often for the benefit of the protagonist, helping him or her learn a lesson or advance on a quest. Yet, despite their deep and inextricable involvement in the trajectory of the story, tricksters are usually not directly impacted by the conflict they create and leave other characters to make meaning from their actions.

As a trickster-like figure, Sophia challenges the characterization of the "old lady" as weak, powerless, and inconsequential. Her stereotypical appearance is a cover for subversion like the shapeshifting Loki of Norse mythology. This subversion creates the framework of the trickster and gives her the ability to transgress social boundaries of how elderly women should behave. Sophia shapes her own life by seeking out romantic relationships, friendships, and money that few "old ladies" on television have had the opportunity to do. In this way, she aligns with Landay's description of the female trickster who represents "a threat to social stability with their individualistic pursuit of satisfaction and autonomy" (1998, 29). Sophia receives financial support from Social Security income, Medicare, and her daughter, but she refuses to simply accept only what is given to her or remain subordinate to these institutions. She frequently engages with free enterprise by pursuing money-making schemes like selling sandwiches at construction sites, renting out rooms to vacationers while her roommates are away, and reselling bulk merchandise. She mocks social support systems through parody songs and uses guilt to convince Dorothy to raise her allowance. Unlike Rose, who follows the rules in every way and fails to receive her reward, Sophia often behaves badly but comes out ahead in the end by design.

Still, Sophia is an outsider. She is often excluded from plans or the last to be considered, such as when there are only three tickets to go see Burt Reynolds ("Ladies of the Evening" S02E02). *The Golden Girls* is a show about older women, but Sophia is a full generation older than Dorothy, Blanche, and Rose. They should have very little in common with Sophia, but she is both a maternal role model and one of the gals. She pursues sexual and romantic relationships with men, from a one-night fling with senior heartthrob Tony Delvecchio (Cesar Romero, "Girls

Just Wanna Have Fun before They Die" S06E10) to marrying her old friend Max Weinstock (Jack Gilford, "Sophia's Wedding: Part II" S04E06/07), and even forcing a love triangle when she dates Blanche's boyfriend Fidel Santiago (Henry Darrow, "Yes, We Have No Havanas" S04E01). Sophia instigates many B plots in the series that end up resolving the main conflict. This fluidity between main subject of the action to chaotic side character can be attributed to the use of storytelling as a central tenet of Sophia's character. She moves in and out of contexts and storylines and changes her personality when required for the sake of completing the narrative. *The Golden Girls* begins and ends with Dorothy, but it is Sophia who drives the action of the series. As a trickster figure, she acts as the social and moral compass of the show, guiding the other characters toward the lessons that make each episode possible. Like many trickster characters, Sophia uses storytelling as the primary driver of her mischief. Her "Picture it, Sicily . . ." catchphrase differs from Rose's St. Olaf stories because her listeners expect to learn a lesson or have their opinion swayed when making a decision even though these stories often turn out to be complete fiction.

> Let me tell you a story. Sicily. 1912. Picture this. Two young girls, best friends, who share three things: a pizza recipe, some dough and a dream. Everything is going great until one day a fast-talking pepperoni salesman gallops into town. Of course, both girls are impressed. He dates one one night, the other the next night. Pretty soon, he drives a wedge between them. Before you know it, the pizza suffers, the business suffers, the friendship suffers. The girls part company and head for America, never to see one another again. Rose, one of those girls was me. The other one you probably know as Mama Celeste.

The live studio audience erupts in laughter at the punchline reveal in this story from "The Triangle" (S01E05) because

"Mama Celeste" is the fictional name of a popular frozen pizza brand. Sophia's stories are captivating and full of realistic details and often involve themes of immigration, overcoming economic hardship, and the differences between life in America and life in Sicily. Sophia's stories also frequently cross the threshold of absolute truth and instead use historical allegory to make a point. She tells tall tales about knowing foreign dignitaries and celebrities like Winston Churchill, Golda Meir, Sigmund Freud, and Pablo Picasso.

Because Sophia is able to weave in and out of the story so efficiently, the value of her presence often goes unnoticed. "The Days and Nights of Sophia Petrillo" (S04E02) begins with Dorothy, Blanche, and Rose discussing Sophia's seemingly simple plans for the day—a trip to the grocery store to buy a

The theatrical set is such that the four women of the ensemble cannot be seated at the kitchen table at the same time. Sophia is often left sitting at the island alone. "An Illegitimate Concern" (S05E18)

nectarine. "At eighty-two, that's life—a round trip on the number six bus to buy a nectarine," she says. Rose suggests that having so little to do during the day is sad, and Sophia disagrees. "Not sad. Life. Sad is when you have to mash the nectarine with a fork." This quick, sardonic wisdom is typical for Sophia, who often uses self-deprecating humor to deflect other characters' anxieties about her age. After she leaves, the women continue to talk about the need for her to have more structured activities and that loneliness is a real quality of life concern. Meanwhile, the next scene catches up with Sophia in a grocery store arguing with the produce clerk about the ripeness of the nectarines they have for sale. The clerk leaves to find a suitable nectarine for Sophia just as one of her friends arrives. The unnamed friend asks Sophia if the clerk is giving her a hard time. She replies, "No, I can't pick out a decent nectarine. This way they do it for me." Sophia creates an imaginary conflict to satisfy her own desires. Then, when her friend describes needing help returning a bad lamb chop, Sophia takes up the cause. She poses as the "past president and legal counsel" of NOPRL, the "Network of Older People Retired but Living," and says she is investigating a claim of age discrimination. She causes a scene, loudly and demonstratively threatening a class action lawsuit and a full boycott of the store until the store manager caves and offers her friend a full $1.17 refund.

The episode continues cutting back and forth between Dorothy, Blanche, and Rose at the kitchen table and Sophia going about her day. While the other women just continue to eat, talk about sex, and worry about Sophia's lack of an active social life, Sophia leads a ladies' charity brass band in the park and volunteers at the hospital. She even gives her nectarine to a sick child. Sophia returns home to find that her friends, who were supposed to clean the garage while she was gone, are already dressed for bed. Rose claims they took care of some odds and ends around the house and asked Sophia what she did today. "What did I do today? What I do every day—I

Sophia raising a ruckus over nectarines and bad lamb chops at the supermarket. "The Days and Nights of Sophia Petrillo" (S04E02)

bought a nectarine." The episode ends on this line, a poignant callback that makes us reconsider what we know about Sophia's life and, by extension, the life of any elderly person in our own lives. Even in the vignettes that show Sophia leading the brass band and volunteering at the hospital, the audience sees that she is much more active than even this episode alone leads us to believe. When Esther, the band's trumpet player, asks if she wants to come to art class, Sophia declines and says, "It's my day at the hospital." She is a regular volunteer, and the hospital scene makes it clear that she has a long-standing comradery with several of the patients like Leonard, who comes up to the desk and asks if there are any flowers for him. Sophia replies, "You ask me every day if I have flowers for you, and the answer is always no." Then, she sees a cart of flowers and balloons left next to the volunteer desk. "Oh, wait a minute. I made a mistake. There are flowers for you today." Like the trickery of pretending to be from the advocacy agency, this lie benefits Leonard but disadvantages all of the people who, presumably, will not have their flowers delivered. Viewers are let in on the secret knowledge of Sophia's daily whereabouts, while the other women continually worry about her well-being. Her everyday actions impact people in many different contexts, while Dorothy, Rose, and Blanche become victims of their own hypocrisy.

Sophia as trickster extends beyond the day-to-day narrative of the women's lives into plotlines that address important issues facing elderly women. Sophia crosses the boundary between public and private spheres due to her active social life, and so she experiences aging from the perspective of someone cared for by family at home and also bears witness to the devastating effects of loneliness and isolation that can occur in a retirement community or nursing home. She often references days spent with friends at the community center and also entertains them at her home. Elderly women without close family, retirement savings, opportunities for employment, and stable housing have fewer options and require more support than middle-aged women who still have some capacity to create their own financial support systems. Despite Sophia's independence, the strain of caring for an elderly parent still affects adult children like Dorothy, who worries constantly about her mother's desire to drive, the quality of her friendships, and medical issues.

In "Older and Wiser" (S06E18), Dorothy needs help caring for Sophia during the work day. Knowing that Sophia would not agree to go to the Cypress Grove retirement community as a day resident, Dorothy makes an arrangement with the facility's administrator, Mr. Porter (Don Lake), to give Sophia the fake role of activities director. Sophia believes that this is an actual job and asks Mr. Porter what her new responsibilities will be. "Basically, you'll pop in the video rental, be a fourth for bridge, a buddy. If you do it well, we'll have trouble telling you from the other residents." Mr. Porter's response suggests that the lives of the residents are not very active, so Sophia arranges more exciting activities for the people she believes to be under her care. Initially, the residents are hostile and do not want their routine disrupted, but soon Dorothy receives a phone call from a disturbed Mr. Porter who claims that Sophia pushed the residents too hard with a "dance-'til-you-drop marathon." Sophia says she recognizes herself in the residents and refuses to "sit here while people are forced to throw in the towel." After Sophia takes the residents on an unauthorized, six-hour trip for cappuccino, Mr. Porter "fires" Sophia from her position and reveals Dorothy's lie. Sophia sulks at home and blames Dorothy for making her feel like an old fool. Ultimately, Sophia returns to Cypress Grove as a day resident and throws a party. She regains her lost enthusiasm when she becomes the party host, even sharing an idea to prank the pizza delivery's thirty-minutes-or-less free policy. Sophia tells the residents that she grew tired of feeling sorry for herself. "They may not have wanted an activities director here, but they've got one." Sophia's ability to cross the boundaries of caretaker and someone who is cared for offers more than just different perspectives on aging. She uses this power to enact change and allow others to reclaim their own autonomous agency while resisting the power structures of institutions like nursing homes.

Sophia is privileged in many ways because she has the vital social support of her family and friends as well as access to financial capital that allows her to live on her own terms. Because of her awareness of what life is like for people both inside and outside these systems, she has the capacity to enact change for marginalized friends. In "Sophia's Choice" (S04E22), Sophia's friend Lillian is forced to move from the infamous Shady Pines nursing home to Sunny Pastures, an institution Sophia calls "the worst nursing home in the city." Dorothy, Blanche, and Rose do not understand why Sophia is so upset, and Dorothy reassures her that as long as Sunny Pastures is appropriately licensed, Lillian will be just fine. Sophia insists that "it's where people wind up

Sophia, "activities director," throws a great party for the residents of Cypress Grove. "Older and Wiser" (S06E18)

when they can't afford a place like Shady Pines. It's the bottom of the barrel." Dorothy still does not understand the dire situation Lillian is in, but she accompanies Sophia to visit her friend. When they return, Rose asks if Sunny Pastures was as bad as Sophia said. "There was crud on the floor, rats in the hallway, and sixty people to every blanket. It wasn't fit for human life. Although, in my village in Sicily, it would have been a two-star motel." Sophia uses hyperbole in her description to reinforce the gravity of Lillian's situation. In the next scene, Rose and Sophia "kidnap" Lillian from Sunny Pastures and bring her to their home under Sophia's care. Dorothy explains later that she called Sunny Pastures to check Lillian out properly for a longer visit, but Sophia continues to believe that her caper saved Lillian from a bad situation for good. She cares for Lillian at home with Dorothy's help, but the task quickly becomes too much for them to handle because Lillian has dementia and requires intensive, around-the-clock care.

Dorothy decides to confront Dan Cummings (Ron Orbach), the administrator of Sunny Pastures, to force him to address the poor conditions at his facility. When Dorothy and Sophia arrive in his office, Dan is already on the phone arguing with a vendor in an office full of stacks of paperwork. Dorothy starts to explain Lillian's situation only to be interrupted by phone call after phone call. He suggests that they fill out complaint forms, and Dorothy insists that Lillian needs help now. Dan explains that Sunny Pastures is understaffed and underfunded and that there is nothing he can do to improve conditions. Social Security and Medicare payments do not cover the entire cost of operations and government subsidies only cover enough of the expenses to meet minimum requirements. Even so, the facility operates at a loss. The administrator's position represents a common challenge faced by nursing home administration across the country: steady increases in capacity combined with budget cuts mean diminished quality of care for all residents.

Dorothy and Sophia return home feeling anxious about Lillian's future and hopeless about the funding crisis. Rose returns home and excitedly breaks the news that she's found a much nicer nursing home for Lillian, but the problem is that her benefits will not cover the whole cost and would need $150 per month to cover the difference. Blanche, who spent the entire episode planning for breast implant surgery, decides to use the money in her "bosom account" to cover the difference for two years so that Lillian can move into the higher-quality nursing home. The issue seems to resolve itself but still leaves the women feeling uneasy. Blanche wonders if their discomfort stems from knowing that the support she was able to provide Lillian is not a typical happy ending. "Is it because we know that Lillian's just plain lucky? That a lot of old people do slip through the cracks and are forgotten? And maybe it may not be too long until we're elderly ourselves?" Blanche's

Dorothy and Sophia versus nursing home bureaucracy, highlighting the real-world issue of underfunded facilities with overworked administrators. "Sophia's Choice" (S04E22)

concerns are valid, and the increasingly deteriorating conditions of nursing home facilities result in more elderly women receiving inadequate care.

Advanced age plays a major role in determining whether elderly women live at home or in a group nursing facility. Statistics from the 1980s show that 4 percent of women between the ages of sixty-five and eighty-four lived in a group nursing facility compared to 27 percent of women age eighty-five and older (Maas 1996, 362). The Centers for Disease Control attributes occupancy increases to population trends including overall growth in the U.S. population after World War I combined with longer residency periods due to improved quality of life, which leads to longer life spans. However, longer life spans also mean increased incidences and severity of chronic illness, so more older women require more specialized care that cannot be provided at home even with the assistance of a home nurse (Decker 2005). Lack of oversight and funding led to serious problems in many retirement communities and nursing homes, suggesting that the plotline of "Never Yell 'Fire' in a Crowded Retirement Home" (S06E24/25), in which Sophia is arrested and questioned on arson charges stemming from her alleged involvement in setting the fire at Shady Pines, may not be too far removed from reality. Between 1952 and 1976, eight multifatality fires killed over 350 nursing home residents. The causes of the fires ranged from faulty wiring to poor monitoring of residents, suggesting lack of attention to the condition of the buildings or lack of adequate fire prevention policies and procedures stemming from inadequate oversight of these facilities (National Fire Protection Association 2003). Police questioning of Sophia ended when it was determined that facility administrators bribed an investigator to falsify the report and she was cleared of all charges. This resolution implies that enforcement of federal regulations in nursing homes is a real-world issue that needs to be addressed.

"Sophia's Choice" aired in 1985, two years before the landmark Omnibus Budget Reconciliation Act (OBRA) of 1987, which set minimum standards of care and rights for residents in long-term, residential care facilities like nursing homes. OBRA '87 responded to "growing public concern with the poor quality of care in too many nursing homes" (Turnham n.d., 2). In 1986, Congress requested a study on the conditions of Medicaid- and Medicare-funded facilities, and the Institute of Medicine received many reports of abuse, neglect, and inadequate care from residents and their families. Disturbingly, the report summary from the Office of the Inspector General indicated that "nearly all respondents indicate abuse is a problem in nursing homes," but reporting differs on the perceived severity of the abuse (Kusserow 1990, ii). In response to this report and growing public concern, the Nursing Home Reform Act and other legislative provisions were rolled into the OBRA '87 legislation that required federally funded facilities to meet minimum standards including annual inspections and a sustained, strategic focus on residents' physical, emotional, and social well-being (42 U.S. Code § 1395i–3). While the impact this episode might have had on changing legislation cannot be accurately measured, it did bring awareness of issues facing elderly people and their families to a wider audience.

Like "Sophia's Choice," "Not Another Monday" (S05E07) brought serious end-of-life issues to the foreground of popular culture by using Sophia's compassion and humor to make the topic relatable and informative. The episode begins with Sophia and her friend Martha coming in to the house in mourning clothes after attending the funeral of Martha's best friend Lydia. The allegorical B plot has Rose, Blanche, and Dorothy babysitting Frank, a newborn who belongs to a young couple at Rose's church who are going on a weekend camping trip. While her roommates are preoccupied with new life, Sophia faces issues of death. She attends several funerals throughout the course of the show, including burying her son Phil, and even hosts her own wake with Rose's help ("Journey to the Center of Attention" S07E18). Sophia tends to treat death irreverently, sometimes making jokes about the frequency with which her friends die. "You're not cutting up the obituaries, are you? I wanna make sure my canasta game is still on for tomorrow" ("Rose Fights Back" S05E04). But Martha despairs over the loss of her friend and says that Lydia suffered greatly during a long, difficult illness. They both agree that sometimes death can be a blessing, as it ends suffering, but Martha says she still feels distraught. Sophia quips, "Hey, I'm the one who should feel bad. Lydia and I were wearing the same dress." In the next scene, Sophia meets Martha for dinner, and she notices that Martha looks more upbeat. Martha explains, "It's a new attitude—eat, drink and be merry," and tells Sophia she will treat her to a decadent dinner. Martha raises a toast. "To Sophia, whom I hope I can count on." Martha eventually reveals that the idea she is so excited about is that she has decided to kill herself the next night and wants Sophia to be with her at the end of her life. She feels worn out by her chronic illnesses and does not see the point of continuing on when she has so many things wrong with her. Sophia tries to reassure her by commiserating about similar health issues that she and others have. "You can't get into a canasta game unless you have at least two debilitating diseases." Martha explains that she is afraid of the pain and of being alone, and that she feels she lacks the courage "to die by inches." She already has the pills she needs to take and intends to carry out her plan no matter what, and she hopes that Sophia will be there and hold her hand. Sophia stakes a claim by asserting her morality and suggests to Martha that taking death into her own hands is wrong and that she would fight to stay alive. "I'd do anything to stay alive. If my heart stopped beating, I'd want every doctor in town jumping up and down on my chest." Martha puts Sophia in a difficult situation, and for once Sophia does not have a ready answer or a strongly worded opinion. She is confused about whether or not to be there for her friend or defend her position toward life. Sophia usually dispenses advice, but in this episode, she asks for help deciding what to do. Dorothy forbids her from going through with Martha's plan and worries about what will happen when Sophia is left in the room alone after Martha dies. After a short argument and a St. Olaf story from Rose about Gunilla, "St. Olaf's own angel of Death," Sophia decides that she must respect her friend's wishes and leaves to help Martha end her life.

When Sophia arrives at Martha's apartment, Martha tells her that she bought a flawless, ten-carat diamond ring that she wants Sophia to have. Sophia tries once more to talk Martha out of her decision, but she insists she must go through with the plan. Martha has made all of her arrangements including ensuring that she will not have lipstick on her teeth at her funeral.

Sophia reassures her that she will take care of it: "Don't worry. I'll take them out and check them personally." Martha says it is time to go and makes a final check that Sophia will be there to hold her hand. Sophia reassures Martha that she will. As Martha starts to open the pill bottle, Sophia stands up but seems like she is searching for the right thing to say. "Do you remember how we met?" They reminisce about being roommates in the hospital eight years earlier—Sophia with the heart scare and Martha with the gallbladder surgery—and how much they both hated being stuck in the little room because, as Sophia insists, "we wanted to live." Martha argues that life is different for Sophia: "You live with friends and family, holidays and warmth. I hear the silence." Sophia tells Martha that she does not have to be alone—that Martha can come over for dinner and holidays and on Friday nights. Sophia continues to talk to Martha, countering every argument she makes against continuing to live. She finally breaks through to Martha, and the scene ends as they embrace.

Dorothy, who has been worried about her mother all night, is relieved when Sophia arrives home and tells her that Martha changed her mind. Dorothy, Blanche, and Rose go into the living room to greet baby Frank's parents, who have just returned from their camping trip. Alone in the kitchen, Sophia picks up Frank from his stroller: "Listen, you. You're just starting out. You're in for the long haul. Keep your seat belt on; there are lots of twists and turns." Sophia is both narrator and change agent in this episode, allowing Martha to make her own decisions and hearing Dorothy's opinion all the while having her own agenda and making up her own mind as to the right and moral thing to do. She stalls Martha with a story, and this ultimately leads her to reconsider and abandon her suicide plan. Then, when Sophia returns home and Dorothy asks what happened, Sophia says, "She changed her mind." That subtle phrasing gives agency back to Martha instead of claiming any credit for swaying Martha's decision.

Sophia uses storytelling to save her friend Martha's life. "Not Another Monday" (S05E07)

Sophia understands how storytelling can inspire action and deploys this strategy instead of giving direct advice when asked for her opinion on a difficult situation. The role of storytelling as a way to make meaning is a central function of religious and mythological traditions, and stories have been widely recognized for their impact as analytical teaching tools in a wide variety of disciplines. Personal stories make it possible to reflect on past experiences, connect with others, and carry memories into future generations. But for all Sophia's storytelling acumen, there was one story she refused to tell: the story of her arranged first marriage to a village boy named Guido Spirelli. In "That's for Me to Know" (S07E04), Dorothy finds a locked box that belongs to Sophia while creating a family history for the grandchildren. She spends most of the episode trying to open the box and is shocked to discover the secret of Sophia's first marriage.

Sophia explains that she had the marriage annulled and left for America two days later. She also asks Dorothy never to repeat the story. Dorothy says she must in the interest of the family history but records a version that emphasizes Sophia's bravery for "refusing to be thought of as property and demanding instead to marry a man she loved. To do so, she had to leave behind everything she'd ever known. And that is the kind of courage and strength that flows through your veins." Dorothy helps Sophia see that she no longer has to feel ashamed of her story. Instead, her experience is a powerful and lasting legacy shaped through its telling. Sophia sets the example of how stories can be told and reshaped to generate change, and this reverberates throughout the show as *The Golden Girls* responded to important social and cultural issues. For some, the show might always be a typical sitcom devoid of meaningful social commentary or an imperfect attempt to push the boundaries of representation on television. But to tell the story another way—a way that recognizes the possibility that narrative can create meaningful change as it circulates—*The Golden Girls* opens up a third possibility that a sitcom can be both recognizable and revolutionary.

Conclusion

84 *The Golden Girls* has been a part of the television landscape for over thirty-five years during its original network run and through its constant presence in syndication on Lifetime, the Hallmark Channel, TV Land, and Logo. In many ways, *The Golden Girls* was ahead of its time as a show that is comfortingly predictable and easy to watch. Even before binge-watching became part of television culture in the early twenty-first century, networks relied on the show to execute what Jaclyn Cohen, TV Land Senior Vice President of Acquisitions, calls a "Potato Chip Strategy," airing multiple back-to-back episode blocks—sometimes more than once per day—because "the next thing you know, you're on your third episode and you're not going anywhere" (Colucci 2016, 365). Digital streaming services like Hulu, which acquired the rights to the show in 2017, reach new audiences and satisfy nostalgic desires for long-time fans. The same qualities that make the show wildly popular and appealing to fan audiences have also repelled critics and scholars from digging deeper into the show's status as a TV milestone. You know what you are getting with *The Golden Girls*: a classic sitcom full of jokes based on the time-tested formulas from comedic traditions of vaudeville, radio plays, and standup

comedy. And in that way, the show is unremarkable. Yet the show was groundbreaking during its network run because it pushed back against long-established norms of television with a deceptively simple premise: four older women living together as roommates.

The Golden Girls is a TV milestone for the ways in which it subverted expectations of traditional representations of women on television within the constraints of a primetime network sitcom, but there is more work to be done. The majority of research on *The Golden Girls* has been written in the past five years, which suggests there are many possibilities for robust scholarship within emerging interdisciplinary fields that seek to further explore representation on television using classic sitcoms as subjects. This book introduces ways of interpreting the show that move beyond the sitcom as simply reinforcing hegemonic norms by focusing on areas of subversion. Future scholarship that establishes a theoretical foundation for how these ideologies became the basis of comedy can take this work further. For example, *The Golden Girls* contains repeated references to disability and physical deformity that serve to establish a baseline of normalcy to joke about beauty. The characters are bound by idealized bodies and engage with diet culture in a way that disenfranchises rather than empowers. The show is also heavily influenced by whiteness as a construct and features no major characters of color, relying on characters of color to provide comic relief. This same work of establishing a common understanding of the status quo about age, race, sexuality, and other issues of representation can be analyzed in new ways. Further research will attempt to move beyond the question of groundbreaking, milestone status to how the show impacted the next generation of characters, forms, and storytelling techniques on television.

As the television landscape changes to include new digital media forms, so too does the reception of the show. Scholarship from the field of fan studies can help explain how *The Golden Girls* fandom has been taken up as culture-in-progress through new media. For example, the popular handmade craft site Etsy.com lists over 28,000 handmade fan art items with show quotes and original illustrations of Dorothy, Rose, Blanche, and Sophia. *The Golden Girls*–themed social media accounts bring fans together using hashtags like #staygolden and #backinstolaf and invite fans to share favorite episodes and memes. The entire premise of the comedy podcast *Out on the Lanai* hosted by H. Alan Scott and Kerri Doherty is to record their viewing of each episode where they are sometimes joined by original cast members and super fans. Fans appear on late-night television to show off their Bea Arthur tattoos, performers create tribute parodies as drag shows and puppet shows, and chefs host *The Golden Girls*–themed brunches. The fan community around *The Golden Girls* is so vast that the first fan-only cruise was announced in 2019. Commercialization of fandom has resulted in *The Golden Girls* board games, decorative housewares, toys, and "Stay Golden" T-shirts at major commercial retailers. Where else can we go from here?

This book has been a work in progress since 2014, and over the years I worried that *The Golden Girls* fandom would "jump the shark." The years that followed proved that my fear has, so far, been unfounded. I hope that the show continues to delight and inspire new generations of storytellers to make even more profound contributions to television history by picking up where "the Girls" left off. The legacy of *The Golden Girls* as one of the most popular television shows of all time and its status as a TV milestone for subverting the status quo proves that *The Golden Girls* is about so much more than cheesecake.

REFERENCES

Ann, Jean. 2016. "'Back in St. Olaf . . .': Regional Variation in *The Golden Girls*." *Watching TV with a Linguist*. Edited by Kristy Beers Fägersten. Syracuse: Syracuse University Press.

Aronstein, A. J. 2012. "*All in the Family* and the First Gay Sitcom Character." Vulture.com. May 30. http://www.vulture.com/2012/05/all-in-the-family-and-the-first-gay-sitcom-character.html.

Arthur, Bea. 2002. *Bea Arthur on Broadway: Just Between Friends*. DRG. Audio.

Bakhtin, M. M. 2009. *Rabelais and His World*. Translated by Helene Iswolsky. Bloomington: Indiana University Press.

Beale, Lewis. 1992. "An Abortion That Shook Prime Time." *Los Angeles Times*. November 10. http://articles.latimes.com/1992-11-10/entertainment/ca-175_1_maude-s-dilemma.

Berzsenyi, Christyne A. 2010. "*The Golden Girls* Share Signature Stories: Narratives of Aging, Identity, and Communal Desire." *Americana: The Journal of American Popular Culture* (1900–Present) 9, no. 2. MLA International Bibliography, EBSCOhost.

"Big Bea." 1973. *Time*. October 1.

Butler, Judith. 1990. *Gender Trouble: Feminism and the Subversion of Identity*. New York: Routledge.

Colucci, Jim. 2006. *The Q Guide to The Golden Girls*. New York: Alyson Books.

———. 2016. *Golden Girls Forever: An Unauthorized Look behind the Lanai*. New York: Harper Design.

Couric, Katie. 2017. "Exclusive: Betty White on Her 95th Birthday." *Yahoo! Video*. January 12. https://www.youtube.com/watch?v=TxgzgQgOj1A.

de Beauvoir, Simone. 1974. *The Second Sex*. New York: Vintage Books.

Decker, F. H. 2005. "Nursing Homes, 1977–99: What Has Changed, What Has Not?" Hyattsville, MD: National Center for Health Statistics.

Doty, Alexander. 1993. *Making Things Perfectly Queer: Interpreting Mass Culture*. Minneapolis: University of Minnesota Press.

Dow, Bonnie J. 1996. *Prime-time Feminism: Television, Media Culture, and the Women's Movement since 1970*. Philadelphia: University of Pennsylvania Press.

Feldhausen, Adrian E. 2000. "The History of Midwifery and Childbirth in America: A Time Line." *Midwifery Today Online*. https://midwiferytoday.com/web-article/history-midwifery-childbirth-america-time-line/.

Grant, Jo Anna, and Heather L. Hundley. 2007. "Myths of Sex, Love, and Romance of Older Women in *Golden Girls*." In *Critical Thinking about Sex, Love, and Romance in the Mass Media*, edited by Mary-Lou Galican and Debra L. Merskin. Mahwah, NJ: Lawrence Erlbaum Associates.

Hall, Jane. 1986. "Sex and the Senior Girls: NBC's *Golden Girls* Are the Toast of TV with Their Mid-Life Miami Spice." *People* 25, no. 1: 54. Complementary Index, EBSCOhost.

Harmetz, Aljean. 1985. "NBC's '*Golden Girls*' Gambles on Grown-ups." *New York Times*. September 22. https://www.nytimes.com/1985/09/22/arts/nbc-s-golden-girls-gambles-on-grown-ups.html.

Holden, Karen C., and Timothy M. Smeeding. 1990. "The Poor, the Rich, and the Insecure Elderly Caught in Between." *Milbank Quarterly* 68, no. 2: 191–219. doi:10.2307/3350096.

Howe, Neil. 2014. "Are You Born to Be Better Off than Your Parents?" *Forbes*. July 16. https://www.forbes.com/sites/neilhowe/2014/07/16/part-1-generations-in-pursuit-of-the-american-dream/#20a1a8075db0.

Hunt, Stacey Wilson. 2017. "*The Golden Girls* Creators on Finding a New Generation of Fans and Giving George Clooney One of His Earliest Jobs." *Vulture*. March 3. https://www.vulture.com/2017/03/the-golden-girls-creators-on-finding-new-fans.html.

Jermyn, Deborah. 2009. *Sex and the City*. TV Milestones Series. Detroit: Wayne State University Press.

Jones, Gerard. 1993. *Honey, I'm Home!: Sitcoms: Selling the American Dream*. New York: St. Martin's Griffin.

Kaler, Anne K. 1990. "Golden Girls: Feminine Archetypal Patterns of the Complete Woman." *Journal of Popular Culture* 24, no. 3: 49–60.

Kannen, Victoria. 2016. "'This Is Mud on Our Faces! We're Not Really Black!': Teaching Gender, Race, and Age through Humour in *The*

Golden Girls." *Outskirts: Feminisms Along the Edge*. Academic OneFile, EBSCOhost.

Kilday, Gregg. 2009. "Betty White to Receive Lifetime SAG Award." *Hollywood Reporter*. September 5.

Kohen, Yael. 2013. *We Killed: The Rise of Women in American Comedy*. London: Picador.

Küpper, Thomas. 2015. "'Blanche and the Younger Man': Age Mimicry and the Ambivalence of Laughter in *The Golden Girls*." In *Serializing Age: Aging and Old Age in TV Series*, 249–66. Bielefeld, Germany. Transcript. MLA International Bibliography, EBSCOhost.

Kusserow, Richard P. 1990. "Resident Abuse in Nursing Homes." Office of the Inspector General, Department of Health and Human Services. https://oig.hhs.gov/oei/reports/oei-06-88-00360.pdf.

Landay, Lori. 1998. *Madcaps, Screwballs, and Con Women: The Female Trickster in American Culture*. Philadelphia: University of Pennsylvania Press.

Maas, Meridean. 1996. "Nursing Staff and Quality of Care in Nursing Homes." Institute of Medicine. *Nursing Staff in Hospitals and Nursing Homes: Is It Adequate?* Washington, DC: National Academies Press. doi: 10.17226/5151.

Macey, Deborah Ann. 2008. "Ancient Archetypes in Modern Media: A Comparative Analysis of *The Golden Girls*, *Living Single*, and *Sex and the City*." PhD diss., University of Oregon.

Marc, David. 1997. *Comic Visions: Television Comedy and American Culture*. Hoboken, NJ: Wiley-Blackwell.

Mattick, Paul. 1998. "Hotfoots of the Gods." *New York Times Book Review*. February 15. https://archive.nytimes.com/www.nytimes.com/books/98/02/15/reviews/980215.15mattict.html.

Mills, Brett. 2006. *Television Sitcom*. London: British Film Institute.

———. 2009. *The Sitcom*. TV Genres Series. Edinburgh: Edinburgh University Press.

Mittell, Jason. 2010. *Television and American Culture*. New York: Oxford University Press.

National Fire Protection Association. 2003. "Deadliest Fires in Facilities for Older Adults." March. https://www.nfpa.org/News-and-Research/Fire-statistics-and-reports/Fire-statistics/Fires-by-property-type/Health-care-facilities/Deadliest-fires-in-facilities-for-older-adults.

Oberman, Jeffrey. 2016. "How Binge-Watching Creates a New Art Form." *Inroads: A Journal of Opinion*, no. 39: 119–38. General OneFile, EBSCOhost.

Patterson, Eleanor. 2016. "*The Golden Girls* Live: Residual Television Texts, Participatory Culture, and Queering TV Heritage through Drag." *Feminist Media Studies* 16, no. 5: 838–51. MLA International Bibliography, EBSCOhost.

Rowe, Kathleen. 2011. *The Unruly Woman: Gender and the Genres of Laughter*. Austin: University of Texas Press.

Russo, Mary. 1986. "Female Grotesques: Carnival and Theory." In *Feminist Studies/Critical Studies*, 213–29. London: Palgrave Macmillan.

Schechner, Richard. 2002. *Performance Studies: An Introduction*. New York: Routledge.

Schiappa, Edward, et al. 2006. "Can One TV Show Make a Difference? *Will & Grace* and the Parasocial Contact Hypothesis." *Journal of Homosexuality* 51, no. 4: 15–37.

Scott, J. Blake. 2003. *Risky Rhetoric: AIDS and the Cultural Practices of HIV Testing*. Carbondale: Southern Illinois University Press.

Sedita, Scott. 2014. *The Eight Characters of Comedy: Guide to Sitcom Acting and Writing*. Los Angeles: Atides Publishing.

Timmerman, Sandra. 2005. "Retirement Income Decisions: The Silent Generation Speaks." *Benefits Quarterly* 30. General OneFile, EBSCOhost.

Turnham, Hollis. n.d. "OBRA '87 Summary." North Carolina Department of Health and Human Services.

Van Bauwel, Sofie. 2018. "Invisible Golden Girls?: Post-Feminist Discourses and Female Ageing Bodies in Contemporary Television Fiction." *Feminist Media Studies* 18, no. 1: 21–33. MLA International Bibliography, EBSCOhost.

Westcott, Kathryn. 2011. "Why Is the Word 'Slut' So Powerful?" *BBC News Magazine Online*. May 12. https://www.bbc.co.uk/news/magazine-13333013.

White, Betty. 1995. *Here We Go Again: My Life in Television*. New York: Scribner.

White, Mimi. 1987. "Ideological Analysis and Television." In *Channels of Discourse: Television and Contemporary Criticism*, edited by Robert Allen. Chapel Hill: University of North Carolina Press.

Wilder, Darcie. 2017. "I Think about This a Lot: *The Golden Girls* Plotline Where Rose Is Addicted to Pills." *The Cut*. August 21. https://www.thecut.com/2017/08/i-think-about-this-a-lot-golden-girls-rose-drugs.html.

Woodward, Kathleen M., ed. 1999. *Figuring Age: Women, Bodies, Generations*. Bloomington: Indiana University Press.

EPISODES OF *THE GOLDEN GIRLS* REFERENCED

Note: A full episode guide is available from many print and online sources including the Internet Movie Database (imdb.com) and *Golden Girls Forever* (Colucci 2016).

"The Engagement" (S01E01)
"Rose the Prude" (S01E03)
"The Triangle" (S01E05)
"Blanche and the Younger Man" (S01E09)
"That Was No Lady" (S01E14)
"The Truth Will Out" (S01E16)
"Second Motherhood" (S01E19)
"Job Hunting" (S01E22)
"The Way We Met" (S01E25)
"The End of the Curse" (S02E01)
"Ladies of the Evening" (S02E02)
"Take Him, He's Mine" (S02E03)
"Isn't It Romantic?" (S02E05)
"The Actor" (S02E14)
"Son-in-Law Dearest" (S02E23)
"A Piece of Cake" (S02E25)
"Blanche's Little Girl" (S03E14)
"And Ma Makes Three" (S03E20)
"Yes, We Have No Havanas" (S04E01)
"The Days and Nights of Sophia Petrillo" (S04E02)
"Sophia's Wedding: Part II" (S04E06/07)
"Scared Straight" (S04E09)
"High Anxiety" (S04E20)
"Sophia's Choice" (S04E22)

"Foreign Exchange" (S04E24)
"The Accurate Conception" (S05E03)
"Rose Fights Back" (S05E04)
"Not Another Monday" (S05E07)
"An Illegitimate Concern" (S05E18)
"72 Hours" (S05E19)
"Cheaters" (S05E22)
"Blanche Delivers" (S06E01)
"Girls Just Wanna Have Fun before They Die" (S06E10)
"Sister of the Bride" (S06E14)
"Older and Wiser" (S06E18)
"Melodrama" (S06E19)
"Even Grandmas Get the Blues" (S06E20)
"Never Yell 'Fire' in a Crowded Retirement Home" (S06E24/25)
"Henny Penny—Straight, No Chaser" (S06E26)
"That's for Me to Know" (S07E04)
"Old Boyfriends" (S07E14)
"Goodbye, Mr. Gordon" (S07E15)
"The Commitments" (S07E16)
"Journey to the Center of Attention" (S07E18)
"One Flew Out of the Cuckoo's Nest" (S07E25/26)

INDEX

"Accurate Conception, The," 43–44
"Actor, The," 21–22
advertising, 5, 6–7
age and aging. *See also* beauty; body image
  Blanche and cultural and biological processes of, 38–41, 46
  The Golden Girls as subversive interpretation of, 3–4
  and issues facing Sophia and elderly women, 73–82
  and Rose's employment and financial insecurity, 58–59, 60, 61
  and Sophia's daily life, 70–73
AIDS crisis, 61–63
anti-gay prejudice, 62–63. *See also* gay rights and characters; queerness
Arthur, Bea. *See also* Dorothy
  gay rights activism of, 30, 31
  portrayals of Dorothy, 15–16
  role of Dorothy written for, 13
  roles and popularity of, 14–15
assisted suicide, 79–82

Bakhtin, Mikhail, 36–37, 39
beauty. *See also* age and aging; body image
  and Blanche's reactions to cultural and biological processes of aging, 40–41, 46
  Dorothy and redefining of, 23–27
  and gender performativity of Blanche, 38
  reinforcement of stereotypes regarding, 17–19, 85
Berzsenyi, Christyne, 9
binge-watching, 12, 84
Blanche. *See also* McClanahan, Rue
  bond of, with other girls, 54–56
  challenges notion of mother, 37–38
  costuming of, 6
  and cultural and biological processes of aging, 4, 38–41
  gender performativity of, 29
  and gender performativity of Dorothy, 20, 21
  introduction of, to other girls, 53–54
  and issues facing elderly women, 76–77, 81
  labeled as slut, 35–36, 38, 40
  and lesbianism in *The Golden Girls*, 31–32

Blanche (*continued*)
and reinforcement of stereotypes regarding beauty and body image, 17–18
relationship of, with motherhood, 41–48
sexuality of, 23–24, 34–35
and treatment of AIDS crisis, 61–63
as "unruly woman," 37, 48
"Blanche and the Younger Man," 38–39
"Blanche Delivers," 44–45
"Blanche's Little Girl," 42–43
body image. *See also* age and aging; beauty
references to, 85
reinforcement of stereotypes regarding, 17–19
Butler, Judith, 29

carnival, 36–37
character archetypes, 9, 14–15, 67–68, 69, 73
chosen family, 54–56, 57
classic network era, 5
clothing, 6
Coco, 15–16, 30
Cohen, Jaclyn, 84
consumerism, 5, 6–7
Couric, Katie, 49
cultural issues, 56, 58–59, 60–65, 74–83

"Days and Nights of Sophia Petrillo, The," 70–73
death, 79–82
de Beauvoir, Simone, 28–29
Diamond, Selma, 2
Doherty, Kerri, 86
Dorothy. *See also* Arthur, Bea
Arthur's portrayal of, 15–16
bond of, with other girls, 55–56
costuming of, 6, 28
description of, 14
and employment and financial insecurity of older women, 58–60
financial insecurity of, 56
gender complexity of, 29–30
gender performativity enacted by, 18–28, 32–33
and ideologies of cultural aging, 4
insults about looks of, 16, 17–19
introduction of, to other girls, 53–54
and issues facing elderly women, 73–77, 81
and lesbianism in *The Golden Girls*, 31–32
as mother, 42
and "queering" of *The Golden Girls*, 22–23
queerness of, 19
as representing "intelligent warrior goddess" type, 14–15
role of, written for Bea Arthur, 13
romantic relationships of, 16–17
sexual archetype of, 23–24
and slut shaming of Blanche, 35
Doty, Alexander, 31, 32
double aging, 3–4
"doublers," 12
drug abuse, 63–65

employment, 58–59, 60, 61
end-of-life issues, 79–82
"End of the Curse, The," 39–41
"Even Grandmas Get the Blues," 45–46

Fee, Cynthia, 1
female grotesque, 36–37
Fierstein, Harvey, 18, 66
financial security
for older women, 56, 58–59, 60–61
Rose's concerns regarding, 52–53, 55–56, 57–61
"Foreign Exchange," 31–32

gay rights and characters, 30–31. *See also* anti-gay prejudice; queerness
gender identity, 28–29
gender performativity
of Blanche, 29, 38
of Dorothy, 18–28, 32–33
Getty, Estelle. *See also* Sophia
career of, 66
casting of, 66
and *Golden Palace*, 50
Gilligan, Vince, 12
Golden Girls, The
author's analytical approach to, 9–10
as commercial risk, 6–7
ensemble structure of, 8–9
fan community around, 85–86
as functioning within generic television conventions, 4–6
genesis of, 2–3
narrative inconsistencies in, 12
opening credits to, 1, 6
opening scenes of, 1–2
romantic plotlines in, 16
scholarship on, 8, 84, 85–86
sitcom production conventions used in, 6
as subversive interpretation of aging, 3–4
success and popularity of, 7–8
as touchpoint for gay culture, 30–31
as TV milestone, 12, 84–85
"Goodbye, Mr. Gordon," 32
"good girl," versus "slut," 35, 36, 37, 47–48
Gould, Harold, 12
grotesque, 36–37

Harris, Susan, 3, 13
"Henny Penny—Straight, No Chaser," 20
"High Anxiety," 63
Hollywood on Television, 49–50
homelessness, 60–61

"Illegitimate Concern, An," 18–19
"Isn't It Romantic?," 32

Jermyn, Deborah, 5
"Job Hunting," 58–59
Jones, Gerard, 5
"Journey to the Center of Attention," 23–28

Kaler, Anne, 9, 14
Kohen, Yael, 15
Küpper, Thomas, 38

Landay, Lori, 67, 68
Lear, Norman, 13
lesbianism, 31–32. *See also* anti-gay prejudice; LGBTQ rights and characters; queerness
Levin, Charles, 30
LGBTQ rights and characters, 30–31. *See also* anti-gay prejudice; queerness

Marc, David, 8
Mary Tyler Moore Show, The, 15

masculinity, Dorothy's performance of, 18–28
Maude, 13, 14–15
McClanahan, Rue, 34, 50, 52. *See also* Blanche
"Melodrama," 61
menopause, 39–41
Miami Nice, 2–3
Miami Vice, 2
Mills, Brett, 4, 5, 8
mother(s) / motherhood
  Blanche challenges notion of, 37–38
  and Blanche's reactions to cultural and biological processes of aging, 38–41
  Blanche's relationship with, 41–48
  Dorothy, Sophia, and Rose as, 42

"Never Yell 'Fire' in a Crowded Retirement Home," 78
normalcy, reinforcement of stereotypes regarding, 17–19, 85
"Not Another Monday," 79–82
nursing homes, 74–79

"Old Boyfriends," 35–36
"Older and Wiser," 73–74
Omnibus Budget Reconciliation Act (OBRA, 1987), 78–79
Out on the Lanai, 86

Patterson, Eleanor, 22, 28
"Piece of Cake, A," 59–61
"Potato Chip Strategy," 84
poverty, 60–61
prescription drug abuse, 63–65

queerness. *See also* anti-gay prejudice; LGBTQ rights and characters
  and gender performativity of Dorothy, 19, 22–23, 28
  and lesbianism in *The Golden Girls*, 31–32

retirement communities, 74–79
Rose. *See also* White, Betty
  bond of, with other girls, 54–56
  costuming of, 6
  description of, 51–52
  family values of, 57–58
  financial insecurity of, 52–53, 55–56, 57–61
  and gender performativity of Dorothy, 20, 21
  introduction of, to other girls, 53–54
  and issues facing elderly women, 76, 81
  and lesbianism in *The Golden Girls*, 31–32
  as mother, 42
  and political and cultural issues, 61–65
  and reinforcement of stereotypes regarding beauty and body image, 17–18
  sexuality of, 35–36
  and slut shaming of Blanche, 40
"Rose Fights Back," 59
Rowe, Kathleen, 37
Russo, Mary, 36–37

Sandrich, Jay, 52
Schechner, Richard, 28
Schulman, Paul, 7
Scott, H. Alan, 86
"Second Motherhood," 41
"72 Hours," 61–63
Sicily stories, 69–70, 81–82
Silent Generation, 11, 53, 59–60

sitcoms
as commercial programs, 5, 6–7
complexities of, 8
elements in *The Golden Girls* as conventions of, 6
scholarship on, 4–5
"slut" and slut shaming, 35–37, 38, 40, 47–48
social issues, 56, 58–59, 60–65, 74–83
"Son-in-Law Dearest," 35
Sophia. *See also* Getty, Estelle
ability of, to effect change for marginalized friends, 74–77
casting for, 66
costuming of, 6, 66
description of, 66–67
as driver of action, 69–70
and employment and financial insecurity of older women, 59–60
and gender performativity of Dorothy, 20
and issues facing elderly women, 73–82
and lesbianism in *The Golden Girls*, 31–32
and life of elderly people, 70–73
maternal and romantic relationships of, 68–69
as mother, 42
as outsider, 68
and reinforcement of stereotypes regarding beauty and body image, 17, 18–19
and storytelling, 69–70, 81–82
as trickster, 67–68, 69, 73
"Sophia's Choice," 74–77, 78
Stephenson, Ed, 6
St. Olaf stories, 51
storytelling, 51, 69–70, 81–82
Stritch, Elaine, 13
substance abuse, 63–65
suicide, assisted, 79–82

Tartikoff, Brandon, 2–3
"Thank You for Being a Friend," 1
"That's for Me to Know," 54–55, 82–83
Thomas, Tony, 2, 3
"Triangle, The," 69–70
trickster archetype, 67–68, 69, 73
"Truth Will Out, The," 57–58
Turkey Lurkey, 20

"unruly woman," Blanche as, 37, 48

"Way We Met, The," 53–54
White, Betty. *See also* Rose
career of, 49–51
and portrayal of Rose, 52
White, Mimi, 31, 32
wikis, 12
Wilder, Darcie, 64
Witt, Paul, 2
Woodward, Kathleen, 3

ABOUT THE AUTHOR

Kate Browne is a culture writer and essayist. She holds a PhD in English studies from Illinois State University and teaches about pop culture and body image both in and out of the classroom. Kate is also the founder of Taking Up Space, a blog about marketing tactics in the health, wellness, and fitness industries.